Skills for

BRITISH AND EUROPEAN HISTORY

GCSE History Companions

PHILIP SAUVAIN

STANLEY THORNES (PUBLISHERS) LTD

Text © Philip Sauvain, 1988
Original line artwork © Stanley Thornes (Publishers) Ltd, 1988

First published in 1988 by:
Stanley Thornes (Publishers) Ltd
Old Station Drive
Leckhampton
CHELTENHAM GL53 0DN
England

British Library Cataloguing in Publication Data

Sauvain, Philip, 1933–
    Skills for British and European history
    — (GCSE history companions).
    1. Europe. Historiology
    I. Title   II. Series
    940′.072

    ISBN 0-85950-827-7

Cover illustration: The Charge of the Light Brigade, 25 October 1854, drawn by W. Simpson, reproduced by kind permission of BBC Hulton Picture Library.

Typeset by Tech-Set, Gateshead, Tyne & Wear
in 10½/12½ Times
Printed and bound in Great Britain at The Bath Press, Avon

Contents

Acknowledgements

The author and publishers are grateful to the following for supplying and giving permission to reproduce illustrative material:

BBC Hulton Picture Library, pages 11, 34, 45, 102 (right); Bettmann Archive, page 7 (below); British Library, page 57; Bundesarchiv, page 68; Daily Mail for extracts from the *Daily Chronicle* and *Daily Mail*, page 61; David King Collection, page 88 (above); Essex County Record Office, page 89; Fitzroy Collection, page 69 (right); The Hamlyn Publishing Group, page 91; *Illustrated London News*, pages 78, 112; Imperial War Museum, pages 103, 109, 111 (above and below); Keystone, page 55; Mansell Collection, pages 76, 87, 102 (left); Mary Evans Picture Library, page 104; Musée de Versailles, page 13; Popperfoto, pages 8 (above), 92; Sport & General Press Agency, page 94; Syndication International, page 70; TUC, page 37 (left) and extract from *The British Worker*, page 61; Weiner Library, page 67.

The author and publishers are also grateful to the following for permission to reproduce poems:

The estate of Wilfred Owen, the estate of C D Lewis and Chatto & Windus for 'The Sentry', page 112; George Sassoon for 'A Working Party' page 110.

Introduction

OUR LINKS WITH THE PAST

In 1983 *The Sunday Times* carried a report in which a journalist wrote:

> Last Tuesday I shook hands with a man who, when he was two, shook hands with a soldier who fought at the battle of Waterloo. For a moment I touched history.

Links with the past like this can be experienced every day. Your great grandmother knew people who lived at the time of the Crimean War from 1854 to 1856. She had a great grandmother herself who might have travelled in a stage coach in the 1820s or cheered when news of Nelson's victory at Trafalgar reached her town in 1805!

You can see and touch the past in the buildings and monuments near your home. Churches, castles, abbeys, mansions, houses, mills, paintings and photographs show us what buildings and people looked like in the past. Documents, books and newspapers also tell us what happened in the past. We call this *historical evidence*.

We need to know about the past in order to understand the present. Only if we find out about the history of European colonialism in Africa can we explain why the policy of apartheid was introduced and why it has isolated South Africa from the rest of the world today. Only if we know something of the history of Ireland can we begin to understand the different attitudes taken by people in Northern Ireland and the Irish Republic today.

Police marching into the Shankill Road during the 'No Home Rule' riots in Belfast in 1886

With many of the topics you study in British and European history you will find a local link with the past. Blocked-up windows in an old building may remind you that many people in Britain bricked up their windows rather than pay Window Tax in the years before 1851 (when it was repealed). House, street and place names, such as Waterloo Road, Sebastopol Terrace, Ladysmith House, Palmerston Road, Nelson, and King George V Avenue, recall some of the events and personalities of the past. Statues, memorials, inn signs and house plaques may link your town directly to topics such as the Napoleonic Wars, the scramble for Africa or the Great War.

Statue of the Duke of Wellington in Edinburgh

This Tablet
is the last sad offering of
the purest conjugal Affection
to the memory of
RAWSON HART BODDAM Esqr
(late of Capel House, Enfield Middlesex)
interred beneath
who died at Bath on the 20th of May 1812
aged 78 Years.
In his early Youth he entered into the
Civil Service of the East India Company,
Anno Dom: 1752;
and having, through a course of the
most zealous Devotion to the Interest
of that great Body
assiduously promoted
the honor of his KING and COUNTRY,
was in testimony of
his distinguished Merits appointed
GOVERNOR of BOMBAY AD 1784,

Plaque in Bath Abbey to an eighteenth-century Governor of Bombay

Checklist — **The Link with the Past**

Go through this checklist when you start a new topic in British and European history.

1   *Find out if there are any features, such as buildings, monuments, street names or house names near your home which link up in some way with the topic.*

2   *Which of your living relatives (if any) were alive for part of the time covered by the topic? What do they remember about this period?*

3   *What things from the past can you find in your local museum or library which link up with this topic?*

Going through the Checklist

Suppose you are studying the topic of 'The Great War from 1914 to 1918'. This is how you might go through the checklist.

1   *Find out if there are any features, such as buildings, monuments, street names or house names near your home which link up in some way with the topic.*

You will almost certainly find many war memorials in your home district. Some may depict soldiers in uniform or even weapons. You will probably be able to find out the names of the local regiments and the names of many of the local families who lost several of their members in the fighting. Often the Second World War casualties are recorded on the same memorial. You can then compare the effect of the Second World War on your community with that of the First World War.

2   *Which of your living relatives (if any) were alive for part of the time covered by the topic? What do they remember about this period?*

Your great-grandparents may be able to tell you about their experience of the First World War. Ask them if they remember the soldiers, the work done by women in the War, and whether they recall Armistice Day on 11 November 1918.

3   *What things from the past can you find in your local museum or library which link up with this topic?*

You may be able to see First World War uniforms, posters, weapons and photographs in a local museum. You will also find many books in the local library with photographs showing what trench warfare was like at that time.

EXERCISES AND ACTIVITIES

Dates of birth recorded on the fly leaf of a Victorian family bible

1 *Find out the dates of birth and death of your ancestors. Compile a family tree. See if you can discover what part your ancestors played in the events of the past. Did any of them serve in the armed forces? Did any of them emigrate? Were any of them immigrants from another country?*

2 *Find out which of the museums near your home has exhibits which will help you discover more about the history of the period you are studying.*

Testing Historical Evidence

WHAT IS HISTORICAL EVIDENCE?

Historians can use only a few facts of British and European history. This is why they have to select the facts they think are most important, such as the major wars, peace settlements, treaties and Acts of Parliament. These are crucial facts because they affect the relations between countries or have an effect on the lives of ordinary people.

In addition, historians also select a few of the many facts which tell us something about the lives and reactions of ordinary people at the time when these important changes were being made. Facts such as these may include a letter from a soldier who fought at Waterloo, Balaclava, Passchendaele, or on the Normandy beaches. The letter will help us to picture what it was like to fight in an important battle. It may show us the sacrifices which ordinary people had to make. Yet it will not usually contain crucial facts. Similar examples, chosen from the hundreds of other diaries or letters from soldiers serving at the front, could serve equally well to illustrate the terrors and horrors of modern warfare.

Facts are only facts if they can be proved. We need evidence to show that they are facts and not something which a writer has made up. This means that we need to know the source or authority for each fact. Historians divide these historical sources into two main types.

Primary sources always date back to the actual time in the past when the event they record occurred. They are primary sources because they are based on what people saw, or heard, or created at the time. These primary sources may be in the form of words – such as a book, document or letter. They may be in the form of an illustration, such as a painting, engraving, map or photograph. They may also be in the shape of a building, an article of clothing, or some other relic you can touch. Some of these different types of primary source are illustrated on the following pages.

Secondary sources, by contrast, are almost always in either written or pictorial form. They are usually, but not always, produced at some time (often a long time) after the event or period which they describe or portray. The writer of a secondary source, such as a British and European history book, may use primary sources as well as secondary sources to describe events which happened long ago.

The Evening Poſt.

Numb. 1868.

From Tueſday July 18. to Thurſday July 20. 1721.

Since our laſt arriv'd one Mail from Holland, and one from France.

From the Supplement to the Amſterdam Gazette, July 25.

Genoa, July 5.

 HE French Envoy Mſſ. de Chavigny return'd hither on the 29th of laſt Month, and on the 1ſt Inſt. had an Audience of the Doge. Both our Regency and the Miniſter of Great Britain, ſeem inclin'd to refer to the Mediation of that Envoy, the Pretenſions of the Engliſh on Account of the Sums which they ſay are due to them by ſome of our Merchants. Seeing the Britiſh Men of War which block up our Port, and were two Days ago reinforced by two more, have not as Yet made any Repriſals, there is Grounds to hope thoſe Differences will be adjuſted, by the friendly Offices of that Miniſter.

Montpelier, July 4. Tho' we are free from Contagion, ſuch Diſpoſitions are making, as may be of Uſe, in caſe we ſhould be viſited with it. All the Inhabitants of Boutonet, a ſmall Village contiguous to this City, have been turn'd out of their Houſes, which in caſe of need, will be uſed for Infirmaries. Our Biſhop aſſiſts daily at the Council of Health. and has declar'd publickly, that if the Plague reaches this City, he will not only ſell all his Plate, Furniture, &c. but alſo expend his whole Income for Relief of the Sick. That moreover all the firſt Floor of his Palace ſhall be furniſh'd for Lodgings for the Prieſts, and other Perſons attending upon the Patients, whom he will Supply with Victua's and other Neceſſaries, that he will remove to the ſecond and take no Thought for himſelf till he has provided for the Neceſſities of others.

Milan, July. They write from Rome that an Expreſs from Scotland diſpatched by the Adherents of the Pretender, brought a Letter for the Pope, by which they in very Submiſſive Terms entreat the Holy Father, to follow the commendable Example of his Predeceſſor, and protect a forſaken Prince, aſſuring the Pope, that both he and they will always expreſs their Gratitude for it, of which they will give real Proofs if ever that Perſon ſhould recover his Dominions. Whereupon the Sacred Colledge was conven'd, and that Letter read to them by Cardinal Piazza, who repreſented to them on the Part of the Pope, that the Interceſſion of the Scots in behalf of the Pretender, the powerful Recommendation of the late Pope on his Death Bed, and the Intereſt of the Roman Religion, require that a Prince, who is unfortunate on Account of his Religion, be ſupported in all Reſpects, and that for this Purpoſe His Holineſs deſigns not only, not to take off any thing of his former Allowance, but alſo to make an Addition to it, out of his own Privy Purſe. This at firſt was oppoſed, by the Cardinals, who alledg'd, that the Court of Rome did enough in confirming

to him the Poſſeſſion of the Stately Palace the late Pope granted him for his Reſidence, and protecting him openly againſt his Enemies, the Court of Madrid having, moreover, offer'd to bear Part of his Expences, and disburſt the Sums neceſſary for the ſame. However, in a Congregation held ſome time after about the ſame Affair, the Major Part of the Cardinals jump'd into the Pope's Opinion, on Condition, that the Subſidies ſhould not be drawn out of the Treaſure of Sixtus, becauſe neither the Sums borrowed from thence by the Spaniards on Pretence of a War with the Turks, nor thoſe granted to the Pretender to enable him to keep up a Royal Grandeur, have been made good again.

From the Hague Courant, July 25.

Leghorn, July 5. The Maſter of a French Ship has brought Letters from Tunis, dated the twenty firſt of laſt Month, importing, that the Rebellious Giarun Coggia, has defeated the Army of the Bey of Tripoly, and that the latter fearing the Conquerer ſhould force his Way into the City and get himſelf proclaim'd Bey, has ſent his whole Treaſure to Gerbi, intending to fly thither himſelf when he is no longer able to reſiſt.

From the Paris A-la main, July 26.

Paris, July 26. On the 22d Inſtant the King was ſome what indiſpoſed, but His Majeſty is now perfectly recover'd. On the 23d, the Duke de Aumont had an Appoplectick Fit, for which he was blooded twice, and took a Strong Vomit, 'tis much apprehended he can't recover: 'Tis much talked that the Arch Biſhop of Cambray receiv'd Advice Yeſterday from Rome, of his being promoted to the Purple.

Hamburg, July 22.

The Muſcovite Reſident here, has received an Expreſs with Advice, that the Ruſſian General in his late Expedition againſt Sweden landed abundance of Coſſacks, who ravaged and burnt on the Sea ſide near 590 Villages and Manors, and deſtroy'd 12 Iron works. Juſt now a Report is ſpread here, that the King of Sweden is dead, but this News is not credited.

Briſtol, July 17. Yeſterday arrived here the George and Francis from Barbadoes; and juſt now arrived the Oldbury from Monſerat.

London, July 20.

Yeſterday Morning about 3, Sir Jonathan Trelawney, Bart. Lord Biſhop of Wincheſter departed this Life, at his Palace at Chelſea. He was in Nov. 1685 Conſecrated Biſhop of Briſtol, in March 1688-9, tranſlated from Briſt to Exeter. and confirmed April 13, 1689; and in June 1707. he was Tranſlated to the See of Wintor. He was one of the 7 Biſhops that were ſent to the Tower. His Lordſhip is ſucceeded in his Honour of Baronet by his Eldeſt Son, now Sir John Trelawney, Member of Parliment for Leskard in Cornwall.

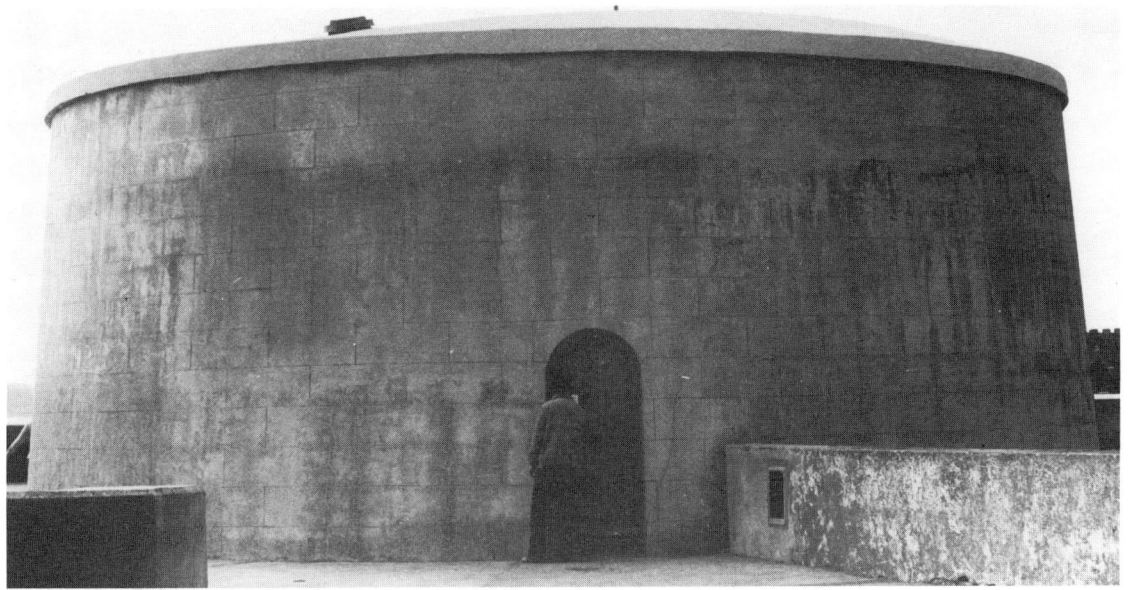

A Martello Tower at Seaford in Sussex. It was erected as a fort and watch tower to guard the English coast against a landing by Napoleon's armies.

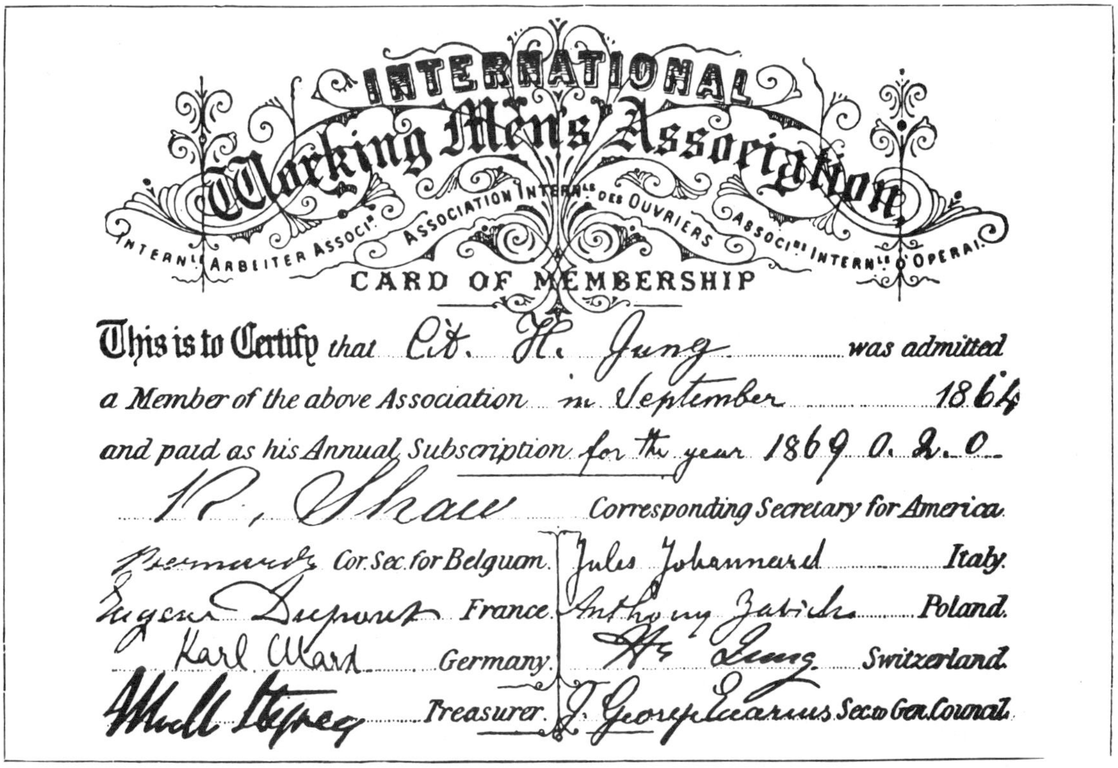

INTERNATIONAL
Working Men's Association
INTERNL. ARBEITER ASSOCN. ASSOCIATION INTERNLE. DES OUVRIERS ASSOCNE. INTERNLE. D'OPERAI.
CARD OF MEMBERSHIP

This is to Certify that Cit. H. Jung was admitted
a Member of the above Association in September 1864
and paid as his Annual Subscription for the year 1869 0. 2. 0
R. Shaw Corresponding Secretary for America.
Bernard Cor. Sec. for Belgium. Jules Johannard Italy.
Eugene Dupont France. Anthony Zabicki Poland.
Karl Marx Germany. H. Jung Switzerland.
Wm. Stepney Treasurer. J. George Eccarius Secy to Gen. Council.

Membership card of the International Working Men's Association signed by Karl Marx in 1869

The Krupp Works in Essen showing vividly the scale of German rearmament before the First World War.

Part of the letter betraying French military secrets to Germany which was falsely supposed to have been written by Captain Alfred Dreyfus, a Jewish army officer in the French army. He was court martialled in 1894. This letter helped to condemn him to degradation and life imprisonment until a public outcry led to his release.

Cartoon which shows the Italian Nationalist Garibaldi helping King Victor Emmanuel to wear a new boot – Italy. Garibaldi was much admired in Britain at this time. The cartoon was published in Punch on 17 November 1860 under the heading 'RIGHT LEG IN THE BOOT AT LAST'. Garibaldi tells the King, 'If it won't go on sire, try a little more powder'. What did the cartoonist mean?

In practice, it is sometimes difficult to say whether something is a primary source or a secondary source, unless you are given plenty of information telling you when, where, why, and how the source was first created. For instance, the sentence – 'The crowd listened in silence; you could have heard a pin drop' – sounds as though it might have been written at the time of the event it is describing. But it could just as easily have been written a hundred years later. A picture may look as if it was drawn on the spot but it could have been drawn many years later by an artist in a studio!

Checklist — **Historical Evidence**

Here are some of the checkpoints you can go through when you see a historical source for the first time.

1   *Can you understand the source? What does it tell you about the past?*

2   *Does it contain abbreviations you have never come across before, references to events or people you do not understand, or words and phrases which we no longer use?*

3   *What type of evidence is it (e.g. a diary entry, a letter, an official report, a book, a cartoon, a photograph)? You can read descriptions of the main types of historical evidence you are most likely to see on pages 49–99.*

4   *Where does the source come from? Can it be trusted? (If you do not know its origin this does not necessarily mean that the source cannot be trusted. We often get information from newspaper articles and reports written by anonymous writers.)*

5   *When was the source created? Was it created within minutes, hours, days, weeks, months or years of the event or happening it portrays?*

6   *Is there any statement, or clue, to show that the source is actually based on the writer's own experience or on events which he or she witnessed? In other words, was the writer in a good position to say what happened?*

7   *If the source was written a long time after the event is there any reason to doubt the accuracy of the facts recalled by the writer?*

8   *Is it a primary or a secondary historical source?*

9   *Was there any particular reason why the source was written? Was it written to please or to annoy anyone? Was it written to justify the writer's actions?*

10   *Are the facts in the source supported by facts you know about from other historical sources?*

Going through the Checklist

Here are two examples of the checklist in action. Notice how checkpoints are ignored if they do not apply to the extract in question.

The battleship Potemkin in the Russian Black Sea port of Odessa

The following extract is taken from a description of the mutiny of the crew of the Russian battleship *Potemkin* on 26 October 1905. It was one of the stirring events which took place during the 1905 Revolution in Russia. The extract comes from an article 'especially written' for *The Strand Magazine* by Lieutenant A. Kovalenko. He was the only Russian officer to join the mutineers. The article was published in *The Strand Magazine* in London in its December issue, 1905. The extract describes how the officers on board the warship were addressed by the leader of the mutinous crew.

SOURCE A

Matushehenko, as if wanting to make sure we were all there, cast a glance around, and then said:

'Gentlemen, the crew of the *Potemkin* have decided to convey you to the shore, but, before doing this, have instructed me to ask whether any of you wish to join the revolutionary sailors, and stand with them for the sacred cause of liberating the whole people from the accursed yoke of the Czar and his Government, to win or die for freedom, as the whole crew has determined to do.'

On this there was a silence . . . I felt my heart thumping against my ribs as great, enormous possibilities rose before my imagination. Perhaps the hour that we had longed for and waited for all this time had at last come, when the armed forces were ready to side with the downtrodden population, and were only waiting for an heroic example to turn their arms against their oppressors and deal the last blow to the hated Russian autocracy. Perhaps the *Potemkin* would be that spark which would light the conflagration of a national revolt to free the people and bring them a better future. . . . It was impossible for me to hesitate. In a moment I had decided that I would throw my lot in with theirs.

A. Kovalenko, 'The Mutiny on the *Potemkin*',
The Strand Magazine, December 1905.

1   *Can you understand the source? What does it tell you about the past?*

It helps to explain the Russian Revolution of 1905 and the reasons for the mutiny on the battleship *Potemkin*. It also tells us that, in the writer's opinion, the Czar's armed forces had to be won over first if a revolution was ever to succeed in Russia.

2   *Does it contain abbreviations you have never come across before, references to events or people you do not understand, or words and phrases which we no longer use?*

'Autocracy' means government by a single person, such as a king or a dictator, with unlimited powers over the people. A 'yoke' is a heavy wooden frame used to harness oxen to a plough.

3   *What type of evidence is it (e.g. a diary entry, a letter, an official report, a book, a cartoon, a photograph)?*

It is a memoir. This means a written or spoken recollection of the past. In this particular case the events were still very fresh in the mind of the writer, since they had taken place less than two months earlier.

4   *Where does the source come from? Can it be trusted?*

It is a memoir written by Lieutenant Kovalenko. He was the only officer to throw in his lot with the mutineers. There is no particular reason to doubt his account, but he was obviously biased in favour of the mutiny, otherwise he would not have joined it. It is also possible (but unlikely) that he had other reasons for joining the mutiny (e.g. fear that the officers were about to be killed by the mutineers).

5   *When was the source created?*

In November 1905, less than two months after the mutiny on the *Potemkin*.

6   *Is there any statement, or clue, to show that the source is actually based on the writer's own experience or on events which he or she witnessed? Was the writer in a good position to say what happened?*

Obviously. He actually quotes the words of the ringleader and tells us his own reaction to these words.

7   *If the source was written a long time after the event is there any reason to doubt the accuracy of the facts recalled by the writer?*

This checkpoint does not apply since it was written a short time after the event.

8   *Is it a primary or a secondary historical source?*

It is a primary historical source since it was written at the time by someone who took part in the event.

9 *Was there any particular reason why the source was written? Was it written to please or to annoy anyone? Was it written to justify the writer's actions?*

Yes – it was obviously written to justify the writer's actions in joining the mutineers.

10 *Are the facts in the source supported by facts you know about from other historical sources?*

In general yes. The mutiny began on 26 October 1905.

The two extracts which follow were written by two English-speaking people who were in France at the outbreak of the French Revolution in 1789.

Oil painting depicting the fall of the Bastille on 14 July 1789. The Governor of the prison, the Marquis de Launay, is shown here under arrest (on the right).

SOURCE B

JULY – Tuesday 14 – This Morning writing. Dress and wait a considerable Time for my Carriage. . . . As soon as it arrives set off for the Temple. Am stopped twice to see if there be any Fire Arms in the Carriage. . . . Return Home late and dine. . . Go to M. Le Couteulx's . . . While sitting here a Person comes in and announces the taking of the Bastile, the Governor of which is beheaded and the Prevost des Marchands is killed and also beheaded; they are carrying the Heads in Triumph thro the City. The carrying of this Citadel is among the most extraordinary Things that I have met with; it cost the Assailants sixty Men it is said.'

Gouverneur Morris (the American Minister to France),
A Diary of the French Revolution,
edited by Beatrix Cary Davenport, Harrap, 1939

SOURCE C

The 20th. To Strasbourg.... On arriving at the inn, hear the interesting news of the revolt of Paris – The *Gardes Françaises* joining the people; the little dependence on the rest of the troops; the taking of the Bastile; and the institution of the *milice bourgeoisie*; in a word of the absolute overthrow of the old government.

Arthur Young, *Travels in France During the Years*
1787, 1788, 1789

1　*Can you understand the sources? What do they tell you about the past?*

They tell us the reaction of two English-speaking people to the news of the fall of the Bastille on 14 July 1789. This is the date which the people of France celebrate each year as the start of the French Revolution. Neither writer appears to be horrified at the news. One describes it as 'most extraordinary' and the other as 'interesting news'. The first source implies that the authorities were aware that something was happening since the Minister's carriage was twice searched for firearms. It took six days for the news to reach Arthur Young in Strasbourg – about 500 kilometres from Paris. The time lag shows clearly that it took a long time for news to travel in 1789.

2　*Do they contain abbreviations you have never come across before, references to events or people you do not understand, or words and phrases which we no longer use?*

A citadel is a stronghold inside a city. Both extracts contain French words or phrases – the *Prevost des Marchands* [Superintendent of Merchants], the *Gardes-Françaises* [French Guards], and the *milice bourgeoisie* [citizens' army]. Foreign words are often left untranslated like this if there is no exact English translation.

3　*What type of evidence is this (e.g. a diary entry, a letter, an official report, a book, a cartoon, a photograph)?*

Both sources come from journals or diaries kept from day to day.

4　*Where do the sources come from? Can they be trusted?*

From published diaries. Both writers were important people. There appears to be no reason to doubt the accuracy with which they reported what they saw and heard.

5　*When were the sources created?*

Source B was written in Paris within a few hours of the fall of the Bastille. Source C was written in Strasbourg six days later.

6　*Is there any statement, or clue, to show that the sources are actually based on the writers' own experience or on events which they witnessed? Were they in a good position to say what happened?*

They are obviously based on what the writers were told by other people. They were not actually present at the fall of the Bastille.

8 *Are these primary or secondary historical sources?*

Primary sources since they were written within hours or days of the fall of the Bastille.

10 *Are the facts in these sources supported by facts you know about from other historical sources?*

Yes.

Checkpoints 7 and 9 do not apply.

EXERCISES AND ACTIVITIES

SOURCE D

On the ever memorable fourteenth of July we find him at Metz, leisurely as any modern tourist inspecting 'what was worth viewing' in the city. A few days later, on reaching Strasburg, he learns the great news: The Bastille has fallen!

Introduction to *Arthur Young's Travels in France*, 1909

1 *Why did the author of the Introduction call it the 'memorable fourteenth of July'? Who was at Metz? What type of source is this? How does it differ from Source C?*

SOURCE E

We ran to the end of the Rue St. Honoré. We here soon perceived an immense crowd proceeding towards the Palais Royal with acceleration of an extraordinary kind, but which sufficiently indicated a joyful event, and, as it approached we saw a flag, some large keys, and a paper elevated on a pole above the crowd, in which was inscribed 'La Bastille est prise et les portes sont ouvertes'. The intelligence of this extraordinary event thus communicated, produced an impression upon the crowd really indescribable. A sudden burst of the most frantic joy instantaneously took place . . . Shouts and shrieks, leaping and embracing, laughter and tears, every sound and every gesture . . . such an instantaneous and unanimous emotion of extreme gladness as I should suppose was never before experienced by human beings . . .

Edward Rigby (a Norwich doctor), *Letters from France.*
[Reprinted in *English Witnesses of the French Revolution*, edited by J. M. Thompson, Basil Blackwell, 1938.]

2 *Use the checklist printed on page 10 to check through this source.*

3 *How does this extract differ from those quoted in Source B (page 13) and Source C (page 14)?*

4 *What do you think 'La Bastille est prise et les portes sont overtes' means?*

5 *Study the painting printed on page 13. Why did Edward Rigby call the taking of the Bastille an 'extraordinary event'? How do you account for the 'Shouts and shrieks, leaping and embracing, laughter and tears'?*

6 *Use the checklist on page 10 to study the newspaper cutting in Source F. Why would you have to take particular care if you wanted to use this information as a historical source?*

SOURCE F

WAR DECLARED ON GERMANY.

Great Britain declared war on Germany at eleven o'clock last night.

[*This, allowing for the difference in time, was midnight in Berlin.*]

The Foreign Office issued the following statement at 12.15 a.m. this morning:—

Owing to the summary rejection by the German Government of the request made by His Majesty's Government for assurances that the neutrality of Belgium would be respected, His Majesty's ambassador in Berlin has received his passports, and His Majesty's Government has declared to the German Government that a state of war exists between Great Britain and Germany as from 11 p.m. on August 4.

GERMANY STRIKES FIRST BLOW.

MINE-LAYER SUNK.

right to break treaties and ravage neutral lands.

THE SPIRIT OF LONDON.

London remains calm, confident, and grim. All day yesterday troops were massing and moving. Crowds were in the streets encouraging the troops, demonstrating loyally before Buckingham Palace, reading eagerly the royal proclamations, couched in the gravest language, calling out the armed forces of the Crown.

The spirit that moves the nation was seen in a rush of offers of military or civil service in defence of the country. A stream of men poured into the various recruiting offices and headquarters. Many doctors with large practices volunteered for service as surgeons with the Fleet.

The spirit showed itself, too, with a subtle and ennobling exaltation when an immense crowd in Birdcage-walk bared their heads as the colours of a regiment of Guards were brought on parade in the barrack square. Only a flag—and the phlegmatic Briton is not used to make displays of emotion before material things. But to-day—a symbol, a sacred thing, a whisper of England's soul, and the London crowd bared their heads.

IN THE CITY.

The great banking houses hummed with activity and the "bank holiday" only meant that there was no paying out and no receiving ' The banks are working at the highest pressure, getting straight and making ready to deal with the financial situation to be disclosed when ordinary business is resumed.

It would surely be well at this juncture if a general moratorium were declared, and if the Bank rate were reduced once more to something like 6 per cent. This, with the suspension of the Bank Act, would do much to restore complete confidence.

THE FOOD SUPPLY.

Mr. Lloyd George announced in the House of Commons the steps which are being taken to insure and safeguard our food supplies. He spoke with quiet confidence. Mr. Asquith announced that steps would shortly be taken for controlling the distribution of supplies

Meanwhile, at the great shops, considerable numbers of foolish persons are

IN SUPREME COMMAND.

SIR J. JELLICOE AT THE HEAD OF THE FLEET.

FIGHTING CAREER.

The Admiralty announced yesterday that, with the approval of the King, Vice-Admiral Sir J. R. Jellicoe has assumed supreme command of the Home Fleets with the acting rank of admiral.

Rear-Admiral Charles E. Madden has been appointed to be his chief of the staff.

It is just a year since Sir John Jellicoe taught Great Britain a lesson by striking hard in the course of manoeuvres at vulnerable points on the east coast.

In a few days, with a force inferior to that opposed to him, he raided Grimsby, the Humber, Sunderland, and Blyth, poured troops ashore, and vexed throughout the entire country a feeling of respect for his ability and of doubt whether an enemy might not repeat his success.

Now it falls to him to avert the danger. Sir John Jellicoe is a clean-shaven, keen-eyed man of the sea, alert, vigorous, and

ADMIRAL SIR JOHN JELLICOE, Commander-in-Chief of the British Home Fleets.

GERMAN FLEET SINKS BRITISH SHIP.

DESTROYED WHILE ENGAGED IN LAYING MINES.

The Government is understood to have received intimation that a British ship has been sunk by the German fleet while engaged in laying mines.

Mine layers are a comparatively new type of craft, introduced in 1907. They are mostly old cruisers adapted for the purpose of planting submarine mines at sea, and there are seven in all in commission.

NO WOUNDED LANDED.

It was stated in a London evening newspaper last night that the wounded from a naval engagement in the North Sea had been landed at Cromarty, in the north of Scotland, and that special trains had been chartered to convey surgeons and nurses from Aberdeen to Cromarty. The Admiralty denied this report last night.

GERMAN CRUISER ATTACKS FRENCH PORT.

ENGAGED BY OUR FLEET IN THE MEDITERRANEAN.

Paris, Tuesday, Aug. 4.

The Governor-General of Algeria reports that at four o'clock this morning a four-funnelled cruiser, thought to be the German cruiser Breslau, discharged eight broadsides at the town of Bona, sixty shells being fired.

One man was killed and some houses were damaged.

She then steamed towards the west, where she is said to have been engaged with the British fleet.—Reuter.

Bona is a fortified town in Algeria.

LATE WAR EDITION.

FIRST BATTLE IN BELGIUM.

DEFEAT OF GERMAN TROOPS REPORTED.

Brussels, Tuesday, Aug. 4.

According to a wireless telegram received here, a rumour is current that an engagement has taken place near Liège between Belgian and German troops.

The Germans, it is added, were driven back. Numbers of Belgians were wounded, and will be brought to Brussels.—Reuter.

SHARP ENGAGEMENTS.

BELGIANS HOLDING THE GERMAN ADVANCE.

Brussels, Tuesday, Aug. 4.

According to the "Patriote," the Germans entered Belgium at 8.40 this morning, advancing in three columns of infantry preceded by Uhlans and Lancers, and crossed the frontier at Gemmenich, Henri Chapelle, and Dolhain. One column advanced as far as Visé, and halted on the right bank of the River Meuse.

The Belgians are defending the passage of the river on the left bank, and have prevented the Germans from throwing a bridge across. Sharp engagements have taken place between the Belgian and German cavalry, and up to the present the Belgians have had the advantage.

The forts of Liège are supporting the Belgian troops. The Germans are compelled to wait for their provision trains to come up. They are threatening to treat peasants who hinder their march without mercy.

The columns which entered Belgium by Henri Chapelle and Dolhain were marching towards the forts of Liège, but their advance was stopped by Belgian troops. The first engagements took place on Tuesday afternoon.—Reuter.

Extract from the front page of the Daily Express, *Wednesday, 5 August 1914*

HAS THE EVIDENCE BEEN ALTERED?

Most of the historical evidence that you will see will probably have been altered in some way. Look at the pictures opposite of the town of Kendal in Cumbria (then in Westmorland). The pictures come from different editions of the same book – a collection of engravings of the Lake District. How has the second picture been altered? What change took place in Kendal in the ten years between 1835 and 1845?

Almost all the extracts you see will form only a very small part of a much bigger whole, such as a small paragraph taken from a newspaper of thirty-two pages, or a few sentences from a 600-page book.

Sometimes the text of the extract may have been altered to make it easier for you to read. Extra punctuation may have been added. Old spellings may have been corrected. Words we no longer use may have had their nearest modern meanings inserted into the extract – often inside square brackets to set them apart from ordinary curved brackets.

In many cases large parts of an extract will have been left out simply because there is not enough space to include the whole of the extract in a book, on an examination paper, or in a collection of historical documents. Often the intervening words and sentences are left out because they are difficult to understand today, irrelevant or just boring! Missing text is sometimes shown by a row of three dots like this: ... This is called an ellipsis (or ellipses if there are more than one). It is usually impossible to tell whether the dots show that just one or two words are missing or whether they indicate that several pages have been left out. In many extracts the ellipses will not be shown, since their inclusion every time a word, phrase, sentence or paragraph is omitted would make the text unreadable.

Engraving of Kendal in a book published in about 1835

Engraving of Kendal in a new edition of the same book published in about 1845

Omitting words, phrases, sentences, or even punctuation marks can alter the meaning of an extract.

One of the most famous examples of this helped to fan the flames which led to the outbreak of the Franco–Prussian War in July 1870.

The French were opposed to the proposal that Prince Leopold (a member of the Hohenzollern Royal Family of Prussia) should succeed to the throne of Spain. Understandably, they did not want Prussian monarchs ruling the countries on either side of France. They let the Prussians know that if King William I did not persuade Prince Leopold to renounce the Spanish throne 'it would be war'. Prussians, like Bismarck, disliked intensely the idea of giving in to the French. Nonetheless, King William I sensibly let the Prince know that there would be serious consequences if he accepted the throne.

On 12 July the French Government heard that the Prince had indeed renounced the throne. The news was greeted by the Paris newspapers and the French Assembly [Parliament] as a great victory. But even this was not sufficient for the Duc de Gramont, the French foreign minister. Foolishly he told Count Benedetti, the French ambassador, to contact the King of Prussia immediately and extract from him a guarantee that he would never again support the candidature of Prince Leopold at any time in the future. Accordingly, Count Benedetti met the King the following morning (13 July) on the Fountain Promenade in the German spa town of Ems where William I was on holiday. The King told Benedetti the good news which he had heard unofficially – that the Prince had renounced the throne (which Benedetti already knew). But the King was offended when the French Ambassador then tried to extract the further guarantee demanded by the Duc de Gramont. He refused the request and later sent a note to his assistant, Abeken, to let Count Bismarck (the German Chancellor) know about this latest development. So Abeken sent this telegram – the Ems Telegram – to Count Bismarck in Berlin.

> His Majesty writes to me [i.e. Abeken] as follows: 'Count Benedetti spoke to me on the promenade, in order to demand from me, finally in a very persistent manner, that I should authorise him to telegraph at once that I bound myself for all future time never again to give my consent if the Hohenzollerns should renew their candidature. I refused at last somewhat sternly, as it is neither right nor possible to undertake engagements of this kind *à tout jamais* [for ever and ever]. Naturally I told him that I had as yet received no news [i.e. officially from the Prince], and as he was earlier informed about Paris and Madrid [i.e. since Benedetti had heard the news already] he could clearly see that my government once more had no hand in the matter.' His Majesty has since received a letter from the Prince. His Majesty having told Count Benedetti that he was awaiting news from the Prince, has decided, with reference to the above demand, upon the representation of Count Eulenburg and myself [i.e. Abeken], not to receive Count

Benedetti again, but only to let him be informed through an aide-de-camp: That His Majesty has now received from the Prince confirmation of the news which Benedetti had already received from Paris, and has nothing further to say to the ambassador. His Majesty leaves it to your Excellency [i.e. Bismarck] whether Benedetti's fresh demand and its rejection should not be at once communicated both to our ambassadors and to the press.

Bismarck did think so. He, and other Prussians who felt they had been insulted by France, were dismayed at the moderate tone of the King's telegram. Bismarck decided to communicate the telegram to the ambassadors and to the press – but in a shortened version. He did not alter the King's words at all, except to change 'I' to 'His Majesty the King' and to alter the tense where necessary (e.g. 'to demand' became 'demanded'). But he did leave out sentences, phrases and words. Bismarck began the published version of the telegram like this in order to explain what had happened:

After the news of the renunciation of the hereditary Prince of Hohenzollern had been officially communicated to the Imperial French Government by the Royal Spanish Government,

He then continued it by shortening the King's telegram (see above) to read like this:

the French Ambassador at Ems further demanded of His Majesty the King that he would authorise him to telegraph to Paris that His Majesty the King bound himself for all future time never again to give his consent if the Hohenzollerns should renew their candidature. His Majesty the King thereupon decided not to receive the French Ambassador again, and had him told by an aide-de-camp in attendance that His Majesty had nothing further to communicate to the Ambassador.

EXERCISES AND ACTIVITIES

1 *Go through the checklist on page 10.*

2 *Compare the two telegrams and pick out the words, phrases and sentences which Bismarck cut out of the original Ems telegram. Why did he leave them out?*

3 *Do you think this shortening of the telegram altered or affected its meaning in any way?*

4 *Bismarck claimed that he shortened the telegram in order to make the King's reply seem much tougher than it really was. Do you think he succeeded?*

Europe seemed to think he did. The publication of the telegram in the official Prussian newspaper, the *North German Gazette*, infuriated the French and mobs marched through the streets of Paris demanding war, singing the 'Marsellaise' and shouting 'To Berlin', 'Vive la France!' Equally, it made most Germans very angry indeed at what they saw as French impertinence. 'This nation [i.e. France] deserves a merciless thrashing,' wrote the wife of the nationalist German composer Richard Wagner. War between the two countries followed within days.

Cartoon published in Punch on 23 July 1870 – the French Emperor Napoleon III is on the left, representing France. His opponent is King William I of Prussia, on the right. Britain, as Britannia, is trying to halt the war. France: 'Pray stand back Madam. You mean well; but this is an old family quarrel and we must fight it out.'

A DUEL TO THE DEATH

FACT OR OPINION?

Events in the past are historical facts because historians have evidence to prove that the events actually happened. Historians always need proof. In many ways they are like lawyers in a law court. They obtain evidence from witnesses. They examine exhibits. They argue. They reach a conclusion or verdict. In a court of law, the judge and the jury try to decide the case on the basis of the facts, not the opinions. So, too, do historians. When the members of a jury reach a decision on the basis of those facts they express an opinion themselves. Most times they are probably right. Sometimes they are wrong. So it is, too, with historians.

Sometimes it is difficult to tell if a statement is fact or opinion. It may be written as if it is a fact. If you know little about the subject you will probably have to accept it as such, unless it is clear that the statement could never be proved or disproved to everyone's satisfaction. For instance, if you read this statement quickly – 'The Victorian middle classes were deeply religious' – you will probably read it as a statement of fact rather than as a statement of an opinion. The writer does not say '*In my opinion* the Victorian middle classes were deeply religious'. Nonetheless, it is an opinion.

In the first place, we cannot be sure exactly who the writer means when he talks about the middle classes. Does he include teachers? Or shopkeepers? In the second place, the phrase – 'deeply religious' – means different things to different people. To some it may mean a strict way of life with family prayers every day. To others it may mean going to a place of worship once a week.

Checklist — **Facts and Opinions**

Use your common sense if you are asked to say whether you think part of an extract is an opinion rather than a fact. Ask yourself:

1   *Which parts of the statement can probably be proved right or wrong? A specific statement, such as the name of a person or place, a date, number or quantity, is something which can be proved, or disproved, as a fact. Either the name, place, date, number or quantity is correct or it is not. The same thing applies to specific events or happenings which can also be easily proved or disproved. Either they did happen or they did not. This is a question of fact and not of opinion.*

2   *Which parts of the statement are obviously opinions and not facts? You can often detect opinions where the writer uses words which have no precise meaning, such as popular, beautiful, deeply, friendly, unpleasant, ugly and unwise. By contrast many words, such as French-speaking, blue, fifty and baker, have factual meanings.*

Bear in mind that opinions are often very useful to a historian because they show what people felt about an issue or an event in the past. But beware of thinking that opinions are facts simply because you agree with them!

Going through the Checklist

Part of the British artillery camp at the siege of Sebastopol, The Illustrated London News, 3 February 1855

Read through the following extract from an account written by a private soldier four days after this picture was published in *The Illustrated London News*. The letter describes conditions in a British camp in the Crimean War during the winter of 1854–5. Then go through the checklist below.

Before Sebastopol. Feb 7, 1855

We dug the inside of the tent fourteen inches [356 mm] deep, which left it tolerably dry, and put a trench round the outside to keep out and carry off the water; and with the warm clothing that has been sent out for us, and the small allowance of rum (which is a principal thing here) we manage to get along better than we expected ... since we came up here we have had no fresh meat, except a few sheep the Sultan sent up, about the size of dogs. Our commissariat is abominably managed. While we are starving on dry sea biscuits, the French have erected bakehouses on the hills which supply the men with fresh bread ... Balaclava is an awful place, up to the knees in dirt and puddle. It would have been a very pretty village had they let it stand as they found it; but they expected to take Sebastopol in a few days, and consequently they knocked down the houses.

Letter from a private soldier, *The Observer*,
4 March 1855.

1   *Which parts of the statement can probably be proved right or wrong?*

Most of the statement is factual in content and could be easily verified – such as the method of erecting a tent and its depth, the digging of a trench, the issue of clothing and rum, the lack of fresh meat, the dry sea biscuits, the French bakehouses, the dirt and puddles in Balaclava, and the demolition of its houses.

2 *Which parts of the statement are obviously opinions and not facts?*

Tolerably dry, *warm* clothing, and *small* allowance of rum (*which is a principal thing here*) have no precise meaning although most observers would probably agree that these are acceptable as statements of fact. Statements which are more obviously opinions than facts include the following:

(a) 'we manage to get along better than we expected'
(b) 'Our commissariat is abominably managed'
(c) 'While we are starving'
(d) 'Balaclava is an awful place'
(e) 'It would have been a very pretty village'.

EXERCISES AND ACTIVITIES

1 *The Balaclava extract has the ring of truth about it because the soldier gives facts to back up his opinions. When he says 'Balaclava is an awful place' he immediately explains why – because it was 'up to the knees in dirt and puddle'. What other examples can you find in the passage where an opinion is immediately backed up by facts?*

Read the following extract carefully and then answer the questions on page 24:

> The Reign of Terror was now duly established – the rowdies swarmed down in large herds to the Place Vendôme. The next day ruffians, with red scarves, steaming of alcohol, paraded in pomp, dragging their cannon after them about the Boulevards, and taunting, as well they might, their fellow citizens with their supineness. . . . The convicts who rule us reply thereto, they have no aggressive intentions towards the Prussians. Thus we are left at the mercy of the mob. They keep guard over us, order us about, and do as they please.
>
> *The Observer*, 26 March 1871.

Communards manning a barricade against government forces during the Paris Commune, The Illustrated London News, *15 April 1871*

2   *Which words in the extract have no precise meaning?*

3   *Which parts of the statement can probably be proved right or wrong?*

4   *Which parts of the statement are obviously opinions and not facts?*

5   *Has this extract any value for someone studying the establishment of the Paris Commune in 1871?*

6   *Does the engraving in* The Illustrated London News *support or contradict the report in* The Observer *which was published three weeks earlier?*

ACCURACY AND RELIABILITY

Most of the extracts which you will see will be far too short for you ever to say with confidence that they are trustworthy and reliable sources of information. On the other hand you may be able to detect mistakes or inaccuracies in an extract which throw some doubt on the reliability of the historical source from which the extract is taken.

Checklist — **Accuracy and Reliability**

Ask yourself these questions.

1   *Are there any obvious mistakes or errors of fact in the extract? We can often test for mistakes by comparing one historical source with another. If there are mistakes it does not necessarily mean that the rest of the source is inaccurate. Nor does it mean that the source has no value. But it does mean that you should exercise some caution in treating the rest of the source as a reliable source of information.*

2   *Have you any reason to think that the facts quoted in the account may give an exaggerated or distorted view of the events which actually occurred?*

3   *Has the author left out any obvious facts which tell a different story from the one conveyed by the extract? Is there any reason to think that they were left out deliberately? (It may be that the author was just unaware or ignorant of these facts or could not have known about them anyway.)*

4   *Has the author used any words or phrases which show that he or she approves or disapproves of a person, an action, or an event? Does the author show any signs of being biased or prejudiced (see pages 28–35)?*

Going through the Checklist

Source A which follows is an extract from a biography of Lloyd George which was first published in 1954. We can test the accuracy and reliability of this statement about the suffragettes by comparing the facts in this extract with those in newspapers published in June 1913 at the time of the incident which it describes (Sources B to F).

SOURCE A

SUFFRAGETTES

The most determined martyr of them all, Miss Emily Davidson, red-haired, green-eyed, half-demented girl, denied the sacrifice of her life when she leapt from an upper floor in Holloway Prison after a hunger-strike, was killed in the end on Derby Day, 1913, when she flung herself under the flying hooves of the King's horse as it led the field, thundering round Tattenham Corner.

Frank Owen, *Tempestuous Journey:*
Lloyd George His Life and Times, Hutchinson, 1954

SOURCE B

ABOYEUR'S DERBY

At Tattenham Corner, and after rounding it, he [Aboyeur] still maintained his place [as leader of the field].

The Times, Thursday 5 June 1913

SOURCE C

NARRATIVES OF SPECTATORS

The general impression of those who saw the incident at close quarters seemed to be that the woman had seized hold of the first horse she could reach – which happened to be the King's – not with the intention of disqualifying any particular horse, but of interfering with and, if possible, spoiling the race as a whole.

The Times, Thursday 5 June 1913

SOURCE D

AN EYEWITNESS

They had just got round the Corner and all had passed but the King's horse, when a woman squeezed through the railings and ran out into the course. She made straight for Anmer, and made a sort of leap for the reins. I think she got hold of them, but it was impossible to say.

Eyewitness account, *Manchester Guardian*,
Thursday 5 June 1913

SOURCE E

DEATH OF MISS DAVISON

Miss Emily Wilding Davison, the suffragist who interfered with the King's horse during the race for the Derby, died in hospital at Epsom at 4.50 yesterday afternoon.

The Times, Monday 9 June 1913

SOURCE F

INQUEST ON EMILY WILDING DAVISON
[Tuesday, 10 June 1913]

Police-sergeant Bunn said he was about twenty yards [18 metres] away from Miss Davison when she rushed out on the course. 'I saw the woman throw her hands up in front of the horses. Some had previously passed her.'

The Coroner, in summing up, said he did not think that Miss Davison aimed at the King's horse in particular but that her intention was to upset the race. The jury would probably dismiss from their minds the idea that she intended to take her life.

The jury returned a verdict of 'Death by misadventure'.

The Suffragette, Friday 13 June 1913

SOURCE G

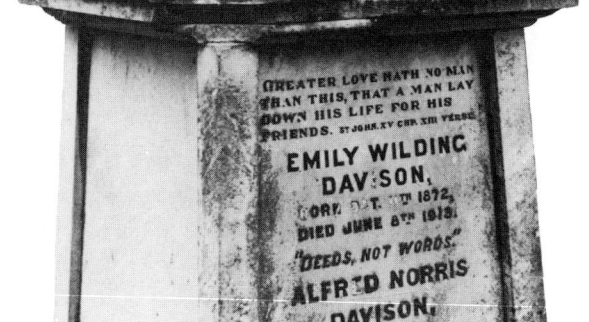

*Tombstone at
Morpeth,
Northumberland*

1 *Are there any obvious mistakes or errors of fact in the extract (i.e. Source A)?*

Yes.

(a) The tombstone (Source G) shows clearly that her surname was Davison not Davidson.

(b) She died in hospital on Sunday 8 June not on Derby Day itself – Wednesday 4 June (Sources E and G).

(c) The King's horse (Anmer) did not lead the field at Tattenham Corner. The eventual winner, a horse called Aboyeur, was the leader (Source B).

2 *Have you any reason to think that the facts in the account may give a distorted view of the events which actually occurred?*

Yes. There is no evidence that 'she flung herself under the flying hooves of the King's horse'. Quite the contrary.

(a) Two of the sources (C and F) indicated that it was sheer accident that she was knocked down by the King's horse. In other words, she did not specifically select the King's horse in order to make her protest.

(b) Far from flinging herself under the horse, one eyewitness (Source D) said she made 'a sort of leap for the reins' and this was confirmed by a police officer at the Inquest (Source F).

3 *Has the author left out any obvious facts which tell a different story from the one conveyed by the extract?*

Yes. The author describes her as 'The most determined martyr of them all' but fails to say that the inquest jury returned a verdict of 'Death by misadventure' (Source F).

4 *Has the author used any words or phrases which show that he or she approves or disapproves of a person, an action, or an event? Does the author show any signs of being biased or prejudiced (see pages 28–35)?*

Yes. The use of the phrase 'half-demented' is intended to suggest that Emily Davison was halfway towards being insane. This was not the verdict of the jury at the inquest (Source F). The use of adjectives such as 'red-haired' and 'green-eyed' can also be interpreted as indicating bias, since they are obviously intended to suggest that she was unbalanced, wilful, headstrong and envious of others. Nor was she a 'girl' (with its implication of inexperience and impetuousness). As you can see from her tombstone (Source G), she was a mature woman of 40 years of age.

EXERCISES AND ACTIVITIES

Look at the following accounts of the same incident (Sources H and I). Both are secondary sources. Test each carefully against the facts you have already noted in Sources B to G. Are these reports accurate and reliable accounts of the incident at the 1913 Derby?

SOURCE H

On Derby Day, 1913, Emily Davidson, a suffragette, threw herself in front of the King's horse and died next day.

G. D. H. Cole and Raymond Postgate,
The Common People, Methuen, 1963

SOURCE I

The most dramatic and most public gesture of the Suffragette campaign occurred on June 4, 1913, when Emily Wilding Davison threw herself in front of the horses as they rounded Tattenham Corner in the Derby. She brought down the King's horse *Anmer*, and injured herself so severely that she died in hospital a few days later.

James Bishop, *Social History of Edwardian Britain*,
Angus and Robertson, 1977

BIAS AND PREJUDICE

Bias in history presents one side of the picture only, such as setting out only those arguments you agree with, or listing only the good or bad points (but not both). It may exaggerate or distort what someone has done or said.

An advertisement is an obvious example of bias. It does not tell you the bad points about a product. Nor does it tell you about better products from other manufacturers!

Similar bias can be found in both primary and secondary historical sources. People often gloss over, or ignore, bad points and the other side of an argument. They may select only those facts which support their case. They may use words designed to make readers feel strongly either for or against a particular point of view. Bias is often political or religious.

A historian must study evidence carefully to see if it is biased in any way. If there is bias, it does not mean the source is valueless. Far from it. The source may be valuable precisely because it reveals the attitudes of a large group of people. It shows how people felt and thought at the time.

Prejudice is an extreme form of bias. Prejudice does not listen to reason. Prejudice can be suspected if a writer is known to have, or reveals, a hatred, dislike, or an unreasonable attitude to particular people or places. This can sometimes happen, even in the writings of well-known historians. Political or religious beliefs, for instance, can sometimes lead to a very biased selection of evidence and lead the writer to a faulty conclusion. Prejudice can often be seen in writings about:

- a particular race of people (e.g. the Arabs or the Jews),
- a particular nation (e.g. the Soviet Union or the United States),
- a person – particularly one with controversial opinions, such as Karl Marx, the founder of modern communism,
- the part played by women in society or in politics,
- a political party (e.g. Communist, Socialist, Conservative),
- a class of people (e.g. upper, middle or working class),
- a minority group,
- a religion,
- a way of life (e.g. that of gypsies).

Bias and prejudice can also be expressed in pictures as well, such as pictures which caricature ethnic groups and foreigners.

You may be able to understand, or even appreciate, why there is bias – such as the bias in favour of Napoleon by a French historian and the bias in favour of Nelson or Wellington by a British historian. Nevertheless it is still bias.

If you see or suspect bias in a historical extract you should treat the whole of the extract with caution. The writer may have allowed bias to alter the way in which certain facts are chosen and other facts left out.

Checklist — **Bias and Prejudice**

Study the source carefully. If possible, compare the facts in the extract with other evidence, including engravings and photographs.

1 *Which words, phrases and sentences seem to you to be opinions rather than facts (see pages 20–4)?*

2 *Are these opinions based on all the facts or only on certain facts which support the opinion in question?*

3 *Does anything in the extract contradict facts which you already know to be true?*

4 *Does the writer appear to take sides by presenting only one side of an argument or by showing only one side in a favourable or unfavourable light?*

5 *Is any part of the extract an obvious lie or exaggeration?*

6 *Has the writer used colourful words or phrases to try to influence the way you feel about the facts? For instance an action may be described as being 'brave' or 'courageous' in one writer's view and 'foolhardy' or 'irresponsible' in an opposing view.*

7 *Are any of the statements controversial? This means anything with which some other people are almost certain to disagree.*

Going through the Checklist

These examples refer to the 'Bloody Sunday' demonstration in Trafalgar Square on Sunday 13 November 1887.

SOURCE A

LONDON 1887

November. The subject which most commands interest just now is the battle of Trafalgar Square on Sunday 13 November. The so-called 'unemployed' & a good contingent of roughs had taken possession of the space round Nelson's Column in Trafalgar Square since the middle of October & had persistently slept there & held meetings assisted by the Socialists & the extreme Radicals ... Sunday, 13th of November arrived, & some Radical & all the Socialist Clubs from all parts of the town set off, followed by the whole criminal population & vast numbers of sightseers, who came to see the fun, – for Trafalgar Square.

Extract from the Journals of Mary, Lady Monkswell,
A Victorian Diarist, edited by the Hon. E. C. F. Collier,
1944

SOURCE B

In November 1887, Cunninghame Graham and Burns vainly attempted to storm Trafalgar Square against the police at the head of the unemployed; Alfred Linnell, the first English Socialist martyr, died of injuries received from the police in the conflict.

G. D. H. Cole and Raymond Postgate,
The Common People, Methuen, 1963

Contemporary drawing by W. B. Wollen showing the Life Guards patrolling Trafalgar Square on 'Bloody Sunday', 13 November 1887

1   *Which words, phrases, and sentences seem to you to be opinions rather than facts (see pages 20–4)?*

EXAMPLE from Source A

The 'battle' of Trafalgar Square. Was it really a 'battle'?

EXAMPLE from Source B

The first English Socialist 'martyr'. Was he really a 'martyr'?

2   *Are these opinions based on all the facts or only on certain facts which support the opinion in question?*

EXAMPLE from Source B

'Alfred Linnell, the first English Socialist martyr, died of injuries received from the police in the conflict.'

The authors do not tell us the Coroner's verdict on Linnell's death; nor do they say whether or not there was an official enquiry into his death. We might suspect bias here.

3 *Does anything in the extract contradict facts which you already know to be true?*

EXAMPLE from Source A

'The so-called "unemployed" '.

The writer obviously does not believe that unemployment was a serious problem in London in 1887. Instead, she casts doubt on whether the 'unemployed' were genuinely unemployed. However, if you have studied this topic in detail you will have found that statistics and newspaper accounts show clearly that unemployment was indeed a serious problem in London in 1887 and one that caused considerable distress amongst the working classes (e.g. children were sent home from school for not paying their weekly penny fees). Lady Monkswell could have seen this for herself if she had read the issue of *The Illustrated London News* from which this picture comes. It was published just two weeks before 'Bloody Sunday'.

'The Poor Helping the Poor: Scene in Trafalgar Square at One a.m., Tuesday, October 18!' A group of *poor people who were employed had collected £3 to buy 'sixty gallons of tea and coffee, and several hundred rations of bread and cheese, which were distributed in Trafalgar Square, during the small hours of the Tuesday morning, to a ravenously eager but perfectly orderly crowd of between four and five hundred persons.'* The Illustrated London News, 29 October 1887.

4   *Does the writer appear to take sides by presenting only one side of an argument or by showing one side only in a favourable or unfavourable light?*

EXAMPLE from Source A

The writer unfairly links the Socialists and Radicals with the 'criminal' classes. She makes no attempt to explain why the Socialists and Radicals took up the cause of the unemployed.

EXAMPLE from Source B

The writers are almost certainly left wing in their sympathies and take sides. They make no attempt to criticise the use of violence by the demonstrators. They call Alfred Linnell a 'Socialist martyr', although people from opposing political parties would be most unlikely to use the word 'martyr' in this context.

5   *Is any part of the extract an obvious lie or exaggeration?*

EXAMPLE from Source A

The phrase – 'the whole criminal population'.

The writer does not mean London's genuine criminals since only a few thieves would have bothered to attend a demonstration by poor people who were unemployed. Instead she uses the phrase as if to suggest that anyone supporting the unemployed must be a 'criminal'.

6   *Has the writer used colourful words or phrases to try to influence the way you feel about the facts?*

EXAMPLE from Source A

Use of the phrase 'a good contingent of roughs' further denigrates the people who supported the cause of the unemployed.

7   *Are any of the statements controversial?*

EXAMPLE from Source B

'Alfred Linnell, the first English Socialist martyr, died of injuries received from the police in the conflict.'

This is almost certainly controversial, since it states as fact that Linnell died at the hands of the police. The authors do not attempt to examine the exact circumstances in which he died (which might or might not support the notion that Linnell was indeed a martyr).

EXERCISES AND ACTIVITIES

The following extracts describe an incident at Llanelli in August 1911 during the national railway strike. Keir Hardie, the author of Source A, was probably the leading figure in the early years of the Labour party. He was first elected to Parliament as an independent Labour member in 1892. David Lloyd George, the Chancellor of the Exchequer, was the most influential member of the Liberal government at that time. Winston Churchill (much later a Conservative prime minister) was then a member of the Liberal party and held the office of Home Secretary. As such he was responsible for the police and for maintaining law and order in England and Wales. It was Churchill who sent the troops to the railway stations during the strike. Randolph Churchill, the author of Source B, was Winston Churchill's son.

SOURCE A

As showing how the troops were likely to be used to shoot men down like dogs, take what happened at Llanelly. A train was stopped by a crowd of strikers squatting down on the line in front of it. Some troops, quartered at the station, rushed up at the double, and lined up on both sides of the engine . . . But for the presence of the soldiers nothing more would have happened. Some boys and youths did pelt stones at the soldiers, and one of them was struck. Mr. Lloyd George spoke of what happened as being undoubtedly a 'very great riot,' and described the engine driver as lying bleeding and helpless from the violence of the mob. This, however, was all imagination without an atom of truth. The train was standing in a deep cutting, and the official story is that stones were coming in showers from both sides. Now, not one pane of glass in the carriage windows was broken, not one passenger was hurt or molested, in fact, they were looking out of the windows, no civilian was struck, no property was damaged; there was no riot. But the officer in command ordered the people to disperse; he gave them one minute in which to do so; at the end of the minute he ordered five shots to be fired which killed two men outright, and wounded four others. John Johns, one of the murdered men, was sitting on the garden wall of his own house in shirt and trousers, looking on; the other was also in his garden at the top of the railway embankment. No one has ever alleged that either of them threw stones or took any part in what little stone throwing there was. Presumably, however, they made good targets, and so were picked off. For the troops are not to fire at random. They are not to use blank cartridge, even by way of warning, they are not to fire over the heads of the people, they are not to fire at the legs of the crowd; their instructions were to make every shot tell, they were to shoot to kill. . . . Hours afterwards when an infuriated crowd were looting, burning, and destroying railway stock, the Major and his men remained immovable until a wagon exploded and killed another four people.

J. Keir Hardie, *Killing No Murder*, 1911

SOURCE B

The railway strike was over, and, wonderful to relate, there was very little bloodshed. The troops fired, when they did fire with great caution and deliberation, usually over the heads of the crowds. Ironically, it was two days after the settlement of the strike that the only fatality from the use of troops occurred. This was at Llanelly, where four people were killed after a train had been held up by rioters, the engine driver had been knocked senseless and looting had begun. This calculated violence by the strikers exceeded anything which had occurred hitherto.... For all the criticism that came Churchill's way from the Labour members of Parliament for his attitude to the use of troops during this strike, there is little doubt that the King's telegram [congratulating Churchill but regretting the 'unfortunate incident at Llanelly'] represented public opinion at the time.

Randolph S. Churchill,
Winston S. Churchill: Young Statesman 1901–1914,
Heinemann, 1967

'Rioting at Llanelly: The smashed windows of the troop train', The Graphic, 26 August 1911. Does this photograph prove or disprove anything in either Source A or Source B?

1 *Read through the extracts carefully and go through the checklists on pages 10 and 29 with each one.*

2 *Why would you immediately suspect that each author might be biased in his account of the incident? How does this affect the way you treat his description of the incident at Llanelli?*

3 *Which parts of these accounts do you think are (a) probably accurate and can be accepted as facts, (b) opinions rather than facts, (c) statements which may be exaggerated or even false, (d) biased or prejudiced in one direction or the other?*

4 *Which do you think are the worst examples of bias in these extracts?*

5 *Compare your answer with those of your friends. Can you be sure that your answer is unbiased?*

6 *Is it possible to think of any source that could have given an unbiased account of what happened at Llanelli?*

7 *Were either of these writers eyewitnesses?*

8   Would it make it less or more likely for an account to be biased if it was written by someone who was not actually an eyewitness? Or would it make no difference at all?

9   Have you enough information to decide for yourself what really happened at Llanelli in August 1911? What other sources might you wish to consult to confirm your opinion or to help you make a judgement?

10 Who was to blame for the loss of life at Llanelli? Was it (a) the strikers, (b) the soldiers, (c) the officer commanding the soldiers, (d) Winston Churchill, (e) the government, (f) the railway companies which held out against the strikers? Give your reasons.

GAPS AND CONTRADICTIONS

As you have seen, historical sources, both primary and secondary, often contradict each other. Differences of opinion are bound to occur but sources also disagree about the significance of important facts and events. They are sometimes inconsistent, even contradicting statements made earlier in the same document.

As you have also seen, a source will sometimes leave out inconvenient facts which do not support the opinions or claims of the writer. There may be large gaps in the records. But note that gaps in a source, such as missing days in a diary, can also occur for very simple reasons, such as absence or ill health.

Checklist — **Gaps and Contradictions**

Here are some of the pointers you can look out for.

1   Does anything in the extract contradict facts which you know about from other sources? Be careful to distinguish between facts and opinions (see pages 20–4). The contradictions between sources may merely reflect different ways of looking at the same evidence. Emily Wilding Davison's actions at Epsom in 1913 (see pages 25–7) were those of a martyr in the eyes of fellow suffragettes and the actions of someone who was 'half-demented' in the eyes of government supporters.

2   Are there any gaps in the evidence – such as missing dates, facts, or personalities – which support a different version of the events recorded by the writer? If so, is there a good reason for this, such as illness or because these other facts were only known at a later date?

3 *Is anything in the extract confusing? Does it contradict another part of the same document, for instance by mixing up dates, or people, or the sequence of events?*

4 *Does the writer seek to take credit for successes which other people claim for themselves? Equally, does the writer put the blame for failures on to other people?*

Going through the Checklist

Read through the following extracts from two long articles published about the London Dock Strike of 1889. The dockers had gone on strike demanding sixpence an hour – the 'dockers' tanner', as it was called. The strike was successful. They got the extra money and an improvement in working conditions. Their success gave a huge boost to the trade union movement in the 1880s. Two of the participants in the strike made a great name for themselves in the trade union and socialist movements. They were Ben Tillett, the author of Source A, and John Burns, the author of Source B.

Hiring dock labourers at the West India Docks. The Illustrated London News, *20 February 1886*

SOURCE A

As secretary of the Dock Labourers' Union and the originator and organizer of the late strike I should like to tell my own story in my own way . . . In the summer of 1887, after twelve years' service on the wharves, I left active work and became the secretary of the 'Tea Coopers and General Labourers' Association,' [later called 'The

Dock Labourers' Union] ... The dock labourers as a class are so poor that the formation of the Union was a very difficult task. We managed, however, after great exertions to collect a band of about 2,500 men.'

A year later he had to leave his job for health reasons and membership of the Union fell.

'However at the time of the strike we mustered 800. [On Monday, 12 August] a deputation came to me with a request that I would place the men's demands as drawn up by themselves before the dock officials, and ask that an answer should be given on the next day.... On Wednesday, August 14th, a general strike was agreed upon, and after a meeting of the South Dock workers, a procession was formed and a visit paid to the gates of the other docks. The enthusiastic shouts of the men soon acted as a call to arms to those working within. From the woodyard of the West India Dock the workers came out in hundreds.... We then marched to the East India Dock, and with added recruits proceeded to the Millwall Dock.... On that day I addressed twelve meetings.

At six o'clock the following morning we were astir and found the ranks of the strikers largely increased. We marched our forces in procession to the West, East, South, Victoria and Albert Docks, and at each dock speeches were made by representatives of the men.... On the third day of the strike we marched, with banners and brass bands, to the number of 10,000 through the City, and a deputation attended at the Dock House to discuss with the directors the points in dispute.... It was during our march to the City on that morning that I first met John Burns, who together with Tom Mann proved such friends to us during the strike....

The suggestion that the strike was the work of socialists and politicians is untrue as it is unfair to the cause of labour. Neither socialism, creed, nor politics entered into the strike. The credit of the victory is due to the men themselves, and not to any speech-making from outsiders.'

Benjamin Tillett, *The English Illustrated Magazine*, November 1889

Ben Tillett

John Burns

SOURCE B

It is now some six years since John Williams, myself, and others, commenced our crusade amongst the dockers ... We who were thus openly agitating and spreading discontent in this neglected corner of the world of labour ... deliberately set ourselves to make the men revolt against their lot.

... An old and settled dock hand, named Harris, appealed to me to form a permanent dock hands' trade union. I consented, and held a meeting of two thousand men, at which many men were enrolled. These were men who had refused to join the old dockers' union, which from one cause and another, had ceased to be worth its name. But the information of the new union forced the old into an activity which it had not theretofore displayed; and of this unwonted activity the immediate outcome was the strike in the South Dock on August 13th. Some 300 men came out, refusing to work any longer for 5d [2p] an hour.

On Wednesday, August 14th, Mr. Mann went down, on a telegraphic summons, to address the men. On the day following I presented myself at the West India Docks, to render what help I could. Discontent was simmering; I spoke to the men, and found them eager and receptive ... This meeting of 4,000 dockers I look back to as the real commencement of the Strike ... on Thursday, Friday, and Saturday, August 15th, 16th and 17th, I spoke thirty-six times – outside of wharves, docks and warehouses, Mr. Mann, Mr. Tillett, and Mr. Champion did as much.

John Burns, *New Review*, October 1889

1 *Does anything in the extract contradict facts which you know about from other sources?*

Ben Tillett claims that he was 'the originator and organizer of the late strike' but John Burns gives the impression that he was responsible and that he looked back to the meeting of 4000 dockers which he addressed on Thursday, 15 August as the 'real commencement of the Strike'. John Burns's statement is an opinion. Ben Tillett's claim is a fact, since he was secretary of the Dock Labourers' Union. But, on his own admission, the union had only 800 members at the start of the strike yet 10 000 dockers marched in procession just three days later.

2 *Are there any gaps in the evidence – such as missing dates, facts, or personalities – which support a different version of the events recorded by the writer?*

Ben Tillett says that on the third day of the Strike (Friday) 10 000 strikers marched through the City of London, and that a deputation negotiated with the employers at Dock House. This was obviously a substantial protest march with 'banners and brass bands' and must have made an impression on Londoners. He also says, 'It was during our march to the City on that morning that I first met John Burns ...' Yet there is no mention of this meeting or of the procession in the account written by John Burns.

3   *Is anything in the extract confusing? Does it contradict another part of the
same document, for instance by mixing up dates, or people, or the
sequence of events?*

John Burns looked back on his meeting of 4000 dockers on Thursday,
15 August as 'the real commencement of the Strike' but earlier he says
that the strike began 'in the South Dock on August 13th. Some 300
men came out.' Even this is contradicted by Ben Tillett who says that,
'On Wednesday, August 14th a general strike was agreed upon, and
after a meeting of the South Dock workers, a procession was
formed.'

4   *Does the writer seek to take credit for successes which other people
claim for themselves? Equally, does the writer put the blame for failures
on to other people?*

Both writers, understandably, seek to take credit for the success of the
Strike – Ben Tillett as organiser of the Dock Labourers' Union, John
Burns as an outside agitator. Each gives the other some credit,
however, but only when coupled with the names of other supporters!
Ben Tillett gives credit as follows: 'John Burns, who together with
Tom Mann proved such friends to us during the Strike', but then he
goes on to say that the 'credit of the victory' was due 'not to any speech-
making from outsiders'. This can only refer to men like John
Burns!

John Burns also gives credit to his rival: 'Mr. Mann, Mr. Tillett and Mr.
Champion did as much', but he also denigrates Tillett's union, 'which
from one cause and another, had ceased to be worth its name'!

EXERCISES AND ACTIVITIES

Read through the extracts from the articles by Ben Tillett and John Burns
again. Go through the checklist for yourself.

1   *What further gaps and contradictions can you find?*

2   *Sum up the ways in which the two accounts disagree. Do they disagree
on matters of fact or on matters of opinion?*

3   *How important were the socialists to the strike, (a) in Ben Tillett's view,
(b) in John Burns's view?*

EYEWITNESSES AND HEARSAY EVIDENCE

Eyewitness evidence can take several different forms. A newspaper report, a broadcast, a diary, a photograph, a letter, a television news report, a newsreel film and a drawing are just some of the different ways in which eyewitnesses have recorded the things they have actually seen or heard. In other words they have witnessed an event or happening with their own eyes and ears. Hence 'eyewitness'. Eyewitnesses can be mistaken but their evidence must be taken seriously if they really were in a position to see or hear something significant.

In a court of law, the evidence from an eyewitness is carefully examined by a judge and by lawyers. It is their job to test the reliability of the witness. They try to make sure that the evidence given is truthful, exact and accurate. They test the witness to make sure that he or she was not mistaken.

In history we cannot question the eyewitnesses who tell us what happened in the past. But we can compare their evidence with other eyewitness accounts and with facts we know about from other sources. We can also use common sense. For instance, how likely is it that someone will have been able to remember the exact words of a conversation which took place fifty years earlier? We ask questions to test the reliability of the evidence to see if the eyewitness can really be believed. Was the eyewitness in a good position to see what happened?

Sometimes a source may give the impression that the writer was an eyewitness when in fact the evidence is really based on a report of the incident which the writer heard from someone else. This is called *hearsay evidence*. Witnesses are not usually allowed to use hearsay evidence in a court of law, since there may be no way of checking whether it is accurate. Hearsay evidence is sometimes used by historians, however, with some reservations. This is because it may have been altered or misunderstood by the person who heard it in the first place. Nonetheless, hearsay evidence is often the only way we have of knowing what went on at a private or secret meeting. For example, you might see something like this in the memoirs of Green:

> I had a long conversation with Black on the 10th. She told me that Brown had stormed out of the Cabinet in a temper.

In other words, Black was the eyewitness *not* Green (i.e. assuming that Black was herself at the Cabinet meeting in question). It would be eyewitness evidence only if Green had been at the Cabinet meeting herself. Instead it is hearsay evidence and cannot be entirely trusted since Black could have heard the report from White and White could have heard it from Grey! We have no way of knowing for certain unless the report is backed up by evidence from another source.

A particular problem with eyewitnesses is the question of when they put their recollections down on paper for the first time or in some other permanent form. You can see a discussion of this in the section on pages 66–7 which deals with memoirs and oral history (spoken recollections of the past).

Although eyewitness evidence has many advantages there is a danger in thinking that an eyewitness must know the truth, or that an eyewitness would not tell a lie. In fact, many eyewitnesses see only a small part of what actually happens. Their evidence is just as liable to bias or distortion as that of writers who were not on the scene at the time of the event.

Checklist — Evidence from Eyewitnesses

1   *Does the source indicate in any way that the eyewitness actually saw or experienced the events recorded? We can often find this out from the evidence itself. Look out for clues in the writing which suggest that the writer was actually present, such as the use of 'I' and 'me' – as in 'I saw', 'I heard', 'a woman next to me', 'I tripped and fell'. Other statements may suggest strongly that the writer was an eyewitness, although they could have come from other sources, such as 'the crowd gasped', 'the smell was overpowering'.*

2   *Does the source indicate in any way that it is wholly or partly based on hearsay evidence?*

3   *Is there any clue to show that the eyewitness was in a good position to see what happened?*

4   *Does the evidence justify the actions of the eyewitness in any way? This does not mean that the evidence cannot be trusted but it does show that the eyewitness is not impartial.*

5   *Are there any other reasons why we may need to treat the evidence of the eyewitness with caution?*

6   *Is there any way of confirming any of the facts described by the eyewitness?*

Going through the Checklist

The following sources from the Crimean War were all written during or shortly after the celebrated Charge of the Light Brigade on 25 October 1854. As you can see from the map on page 42, the British commander, Lord Raglan, occupied a position on a ridge about 200 metres high which overlooked the battlefield. He had a perfect view since he looked down on both the allied and the Russian forces. It did not appear to occur to him that the view of his generals on the battlefield below was much more restricted and often obscured by undulations in the ground and other obstacles. When Lord Raglan on the Heights above Sebastopol saw that Russian troops were beginning to remove some British guns they had captured earlier from the Turks on the Causeway Heights, he sent a written command to Lord Lucan, the General in charge of the British cavalry. An order like this, from a superior officer, must always be obeyed on a battlefield, even if it means certain death. This order had to be carried down the steep hill slope from Raglan's command position to Lord Lucan on the battlefield below. It was taken on horseback by a brilliant but headstrong officer called Captain Lewis Nolan. Nolan despised both Lord Lucan (whom he called 'Lord Look-On') and Lord Cardigan, the commander of the Light Brigade.

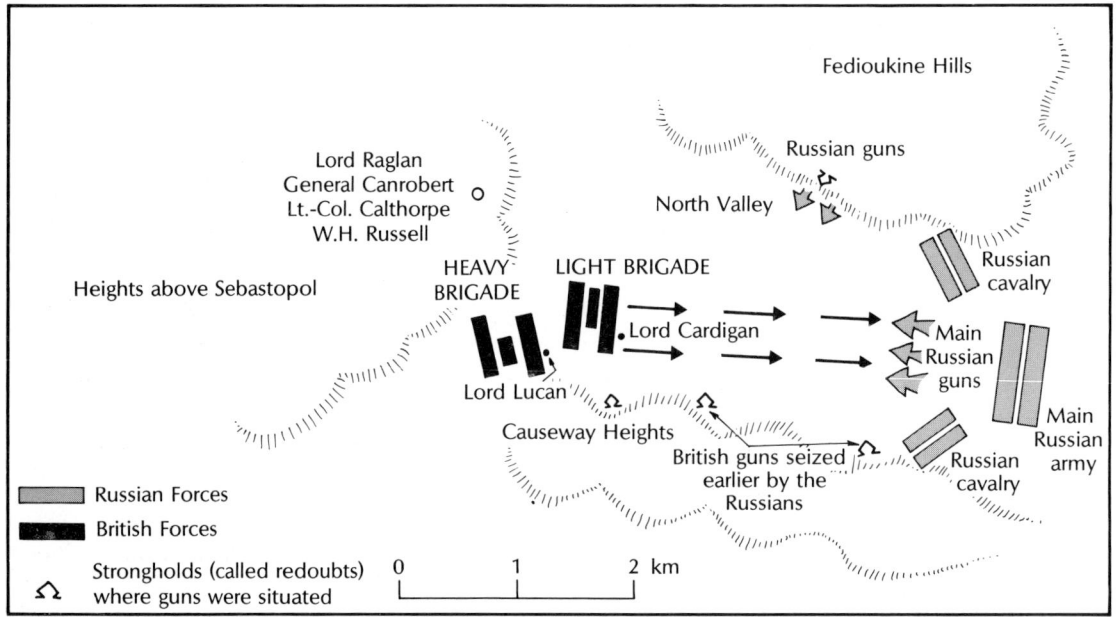

Map showing the positions of the British and Russian forces during the Charge of the Light Brigade.

SOURCE A

LETTER FROM LIEUTENANT-COLONEL S. J. G. CALTHORPE
(one of Lord Raglan's aides-de-camp [assistants] at Balaclava)

It was now shortly after 11.0 a.m. . . . A pause of over half an hour ensued, after the lapse of which time Lord Raglan . . . sent another order to Lord Lucan . . .

'Lord Raglan wishes the cavalry to advance rapidly to the front, follow the enemy, and try to prevent the enemy carrying away the guns. Troop of horse artillery may accompany. French cavalry is on your left. Immediate.'

This order was intrusted, to Captain Nolan aide-de-camp to General Airey. When the order was delivered to Lord Lucan he demurred for a moment to put it into execution, and asked Nolan what it was that he was to attack, who replied, I am told, 'There, my

Lord, is our enemy, and there are our guns;' at the same time pointing down the valley to where the enemy had a battery of eight guns placed as before mentioned, with artillery also on each flank. Captain Nolan appears to have totally misunderstood the instructions he had just before received: 'the guns' in the written order, of course, alluded to those the enemy had captured in the redoubts, and which it was thought they were carrying away; and the direction which he (Nolan) pointed out to Lord Lucan was quite contrary to that intended by Lord Raglan. His manner also was scarcely that in which an aide-de-camp ought to address a general officer, and for which there was no reason or excuse. . . . The fatal order to advance was then given, and, to the horror of all of us on the heights above, we saw our handful of light cavalry advance down towards the Russian batteries. . . . It consisted of scarce 700 horses, although composed of no less than five different regiments. In the first line were four squadrons of the 13th Light Dragoons and 17th Lancers; in the second were four squadrons of the 4th Light Dragoons and 11th Hussars. Again in their rear was one squadron of the 8th Hussars, as a sort of reserve . . . The losses our light cavalry sustained in this brilliant but unfortunate charge were very great. Wounded 122. Killed and missing 156. Total Casualties 278 . . . Shortly after Lord Lucan came up to the Commander-in-Chief, and the first thing Lord Raglan said to him was, 'Why you have lost the Light Brigade!' or words to that effect. Lord Lucan denied this, and said he had only carried out the orders which he had received from Captain Nolan.

Cadogan's Crimea, Hamish Hamilton, 1979

1   *Does the source indicate in any way that the eyewitness actually saw or experienced the events recorded?*

Yes. He says that when the light cavalry began to advance towards the Russian guns it was 'to the horror *of all of us* on the heights above'.

2   *Does the source indicate in any way that it is wholly or partly based on hearsay evidence?*

Partly. When he reports Nolan's answer to Lord Lucan, 'who replied, *I am told*', he confirms what we know already – that he was on the Heights and Nolan and Lucan were on the battlefield. He also quotes Raglan's comment to Lucan after the battle as being 'words to that effect'.

3   *Is there any clue to show that the eyewitness was in a good position to see what happened?*

Yes. He was in a very good position – 'all of us *on the heights above*'.

4   *Does the evidence justify the actions of the eyewitness in any way?*

Not of the eyewitness himself. But Calthorpe was an aide-de-camp to Lord Raglan and can be expected to put Raglan's case rather than Nolan's or Lucan's.

5 *Are there any reasons why we may need to treat the evidence of the eyewitness with caution?*

There are a few minor discrepancies when we compare his evidence with that from some of the other sources which follow on pages 45–8.

(i) From the timings he gives right at the start of the extract the Charge could not have begun before 11.30 a.m. at the very earliest. But W. H. Russell, an experienced journalist who was also on the Heights, gives a precise time – 11.10 a.m. (Source J).

(ii) He describes the cavalry as being in three lines but this contradicts Sources F and J. His description of the line-up of the different regiments in three lines also disagrees with that of an officer who took part in the actual Charge (Source D). But bear in mind that Calthorpe looked down on the action from the Heights (unlike Sources D and F) and he was a serving officer (unlike Source J).

6 *Is there any way of confirming any of the facts described by the eyewitness?*

Yes – by comparing them with those in Sources B–K.

As you look at these other sources in turn, go through the six questions on the checklist in the same way. Make a note of any points where information in one report contradicts information in another, or between the written reports and the pictures.

SOURCE B

Light Brigade in the centre. Main Russian army facing them on the left. Russian guns in a redoubt (stronghold) in the foreground (right).

SOURCE C   REPORT BY THE FRENCH GENERAL CANROBERT

27 October 1854
The English light cavalry, 700 strong, led away by too much
ardour, charged vigorously the whole mass of the Russian army.
After having sabred the gunners of two batteries it was forced to
return, weakened by the loss of 150 men.

SOURCE D   LETTER FROM A LIGHT BRIGADE OFFICER

Camp, near Balaclava, Oct. 27th
You will be glad to hear I am alive after our tremendous affair of
the 25th. We were ordered to charge some Russian batteries and
cavalry, and the light brigade went down, the 17th and 13th
leading in line; the 11th were ordered to hang a little back as a
support, and the 4th and 8th followed, in a sort of third line.

SOURCE E

*Light Brigade in the centre. Main Russian army facing them on the left. Russian guns in a redoubt
(stronghold) in the foreground (right). The French General Bosquet said of the Charge 'C'est magnifique,
mais ce n'est pas la guerre' – 'It is magnificent, but it is not war'.*

SOURCE F   LETTER FROM A NON-COMMISSIONED OFFICER IN THE
                              HEAVY BRIGADE

Camp Balaclava, Oct. 26th
Through God's mercy I have been saved from one of the most
horrible engagements that ever British soldiers were sent into. . . .
About two o'clock Captain Nolan, who was one of Lord Raglan's
aides-de-camp, came galloping down from Sebastopol, his horse
quite blown, and as he rode past, he inquired for Lord Lucan, who
was close by. He said: 'It is Lord Raglan's order that you force the
enemy to retire; there they are – charge them.' Lord Cardigan was
immediately ordered to charge with the light brigade, who took

them up in gallant style in two lines. They had to gallop, I should say, upwards of a mile and a-half [2.4 km]. We [the Heavy Brigade] were the next support . . . The light brigade went so rapidly that we almost lost sight of them, for a more horrible fire was never heard than what was opened upon us. . . . I could see the remains of the light brigade returning, scarcely a mounted man, and dozens of poor fellows crawling along on foot to the rear. Lord Lucan [leading the Heavy Brigade] saw that a great error had been committed, as we were now under the fire of fifty heavy guns . . . In fact, the shot and shell from fifty pieces of cannon . . . was too much for 1,200 cavalry. So we were obliged to retire, which we did with the least confusion, till we got just out of range of their guns . . . after that fatal charge, the light brigade did not bring 100 men out of action, who went upwards of 800 into action.

SOURCE G

Plaque on the house in Penrith, Cumbria, where Trooper William Pearson of the 4th Light Dragoons lived after taking part in the Charge of the Light Brigade

SOURCE H

LETTER FROM A TROOPER IN THE 4TH LIGHT DRAGOONS

Camp, near Sebastopol, Oct. 26th

My regiment (the 4th light dragoons) came from England 300 strong, and now we have not more than 100 left from deaths, from sickness, and killed in battle. . . . I shall never forget the 25th October – shells, bullets, cannon-balls, and swords kept flying around us. I escaped them all, except a slight scar on my nose from the bursting of a shell, and a slight touch on the shoulder from a cannon ball, after it had killed one of our horses; but God be thanked it did not disable me. The Russians fight hard and well, but we will make them yield yet. Dear mother every time I think of my poor comrades it makes my blood run cold, to think how we had to gallop over the poor wounded fellows lying on the field of battle, with anxious looks for assistance – what a sickening scene! . . . Corrie from Pooley-bridge [a village near Penrith], and Bob Mitchell, of Penrith Town-head, are both well. I often think of you, and I am sure you daily pray for my safe return.

SOURCE I

In Memory
LEWIS EDWARD NOLAN
Captain in the 15th or King's Hussars
And A.D.C to Major-General Airey
Quartermaster-General to the Forces
in the Crimea

He Fell at the Head
The Light Cavalry Brigade
In the Charge at Balaclava
On the 25th October 1854
Aged 36

Inscription on a monument to Captain Nolan in Maidstone in Kent

SOURCE J

A REPORT OF THE BATTLE FROM A WAR CORRESPONDENT

October 25

When Lord Lucan received the order from Captain Nolan and had read it, he asked, we are told, 'Where are we to advance to?' Captain Nolan pointed with his finger to the line of the Russians, and said, 'There are the enemy, and there are the guns, sir, before them; it is your duty to take them,' or words to that effect, according to the statements made since his death. Lord Lucan, with reluctance, gave the order to Lord Cardigan to advance upon the guns, conceiving that his orders compelled him to do so. The noble Earl, though he did not shrink, also saw the fearful odds against him.... At 11.10 our Light Cavalry Brigade rushed to the front ... They swept proudly past, glittering in the morning sun in all the pride and splendour of war. We could scarcely believe the evidence of our senses! Surely that handful of men are not going to charge an army in position? ... They advanced in two lines, quickening their pace as they closed towards the enemy. A more fearful spectacle was never witnessed than by those, who without the power to aid, beheld their heroic countrymen rushing to the arms of death.... At 11.35 not a British soldier, except the dead and dying, was left in front of these bloody Muscovite guns. Our loss, as far as it could be ascertained, in killed, wounded and missing at 2 o'clock today, was as follows:

	Went into Action Strong	Returned from Action	Loss
4th Light Dragoons	118	39	79
8th Hussars	104	38	66
11th Hussars	110	25	85
13th Light Dragoons	130	61	69
17th Lancers	145	35	110
	607	198	409

It is not certain that all these are killed, wounded, or missing; many may still come in, and about 80 wounded have already returned.

W. H. Russell, *The Times*, Tuesday 14 November 1854

SOURCE K

A RUSSIAN GENERAL'S REPORT ON THE BATTLE

The English cavalry appeared, more than 2,000 strong.... The enemy made a most obstinate charge ... notwithstanding the well-directed fire from six guns of the light battery No. 7, and that of the men armed with carbines ... In this attack the enemy had more than 400 men killed and sixty wounded, who were picked up on the field of battle, and we made twenty-two prisoners.

Report by Lieutenant-General Liprandi
(Russian Commander-in-Chief), 26 October 1854.

EXERCISES AND ACTIVITIES

1   *How do Sources B and E differ from one another?*

2   *Make a rough copy of Source B and label the different regiments which took part in the Charge of the Light Brigade. Identify its commander, the Earl of Cardigan.*

3   *Use the map to prove that Sources B and E (drawn by British artists) are not eyewitness pictures of the Charge of the Light Brigade.*

4   *How do the different reports contradict one another:*
    (a) about the time of day when the Charge took place?
    (b) about the way in which the different regiments were lined up to charge the Russian army?
    (c) about the losses sustained by the Light Brigade in the battle?
    (d) about the way in which Captain Nolan passed on the order to Lord Lucan?
    (e) about Captain Nolan's position as an aide-de-camp?

5   *Which written sources are contradicted in any way by the pictorial sources B, E and I?*

6   *What evidence might lead you to suggest that the anonymous author of Source H could be the Trooper Pearson who is commemorated in Source G?*

7   *Who do you think was to blame for the loss of the Light Brigade? Was it Raglan, Nolan, Lucan or Cardigan? Or was it just a tragic accident?*

8   *Write your own account of the Charge of the Light Brigade using only information which can be confirmed by some, or all, of the other sources.*

Different Types of Historical Evidence

RELICS FROM THE PAST

Some of the relics from the past which we can see and touch are called *archaeological remains*. Archaeology is the science which studies the past through the materials left behind by people in the past. Much of what we know from archaeology has been discovered by unearthing pottery, tools, bones and the remains of buildings buried in the ground. Thirty years ago people thought of archaeology as being concerned only with prehistory – the period before there were written documents to tell us about past events and past peoples. This has changed. Nowadays archaeologists study the recent past as well as the distant past. Industrial archaeology in particular is concerned with the tools, machines, engines, mills and early factories which marked the beginnings of the Industrial and Agricultural Revolutions.

Checklist — Relics from the Past

Studying the past at a site such as a battlefield, or in a museum, or from photographs, can be a very useful way of backing up what you know about British and European history from other historical sources, such as documents. If you do make such a study this checklist may be useful in helping you to find out more about the subject.

1 *What was the purpose of the object or building you are studying? What was it used for? Why was it built or made?*

2 *Can you date the object or building either exactly or approximately?*

3 *Where is it situated now or where was it found? Where did it come from originally?*

4 *What does it tell us about people in the past?*

Going through the Checklist

Look at these photographs and then work through the checklist.

Fragment from a German Zeppelin located in the porch of Theberton Church in Suffolk

HERE WERE BURIED 16 GERMAN AIRMEN CREW OF ZEPPELIN L 48 17TH JUNE 1917 "WHO ART THOU THAT JUDGEST ANOTHER MANS SERVANT." ROM. XIV-IV.

Memorial plaque in the churchyard at Theberton in Suffolk

1 *What was the purpose of the object or building you are studying? What was it used for? Why was it built or made?*

German airships, or Zeppelins, were used as bombers during the First World War.

2 *Can you date the object or building either exactly or approximately?*

Yes, approximately. It was built before June 1917 – probably in the period 1914–17.

3 *Where is it situated now or where was it found? Where did it come from originally?*

The fragment of the Zeppelin is situated now at Theberton Church in Suffolk close to the place where the Zeppelin crashed in June 1917. It came originally from an airfield in Germany.

4 *What does it tell us about people in the past?*

It tells us that the crew of a Zeppelin consisted of at least 16 airmen. It also shows that people in Britain could still treat their enemies with respect in June 1917 at a time when most families had already lost brothers, fathers, or uncles in the fighting.

EXERCISES AND ACTIVITIES

Look at these photographs of war memorials to British servicemen, built at the end of the First World War. What do these memorials tell you about the First World War? Are there any memorials like these in your town?

Simple wooden crosses from Flanders on a wall in Salisbury Cathedral

War memorial in the centre of Newcastle upon Tyne

Royal Artillery war memorial, Hyde Park Corner, London

DOCUMENTARY EVIDENCE

Anything that is written down on a document (such as a letter), or printed (such as a newspaper), is called *documentary evidence*. It includes wills, Acts of Parliament, advertisements, posters, timetables, receipts, letters, journals, diaries, and anything else in written or printed form.

Last page of the peace treaty granting home rule to the Irish Free State - dated 6 December 1921. The British signatures (on the left) include those of David Lloyd George and Winston Churchill. The Irish signatures (on the right), include those of Arthur Griffith and Michael Collins, leaders of the first Free State government.

The first thing you should do when you see documentary evidence is to read it through carefully to make sure you understand what it means. Then examine it closely to see how far you can trust it as a reliable piece of historical evidence. You can do this with the aid of the master checklist which follows. As you can see, it combines the earlier checklists printed on pages 10 (historical evidence), 21 (facts and opinions), 24 (accuracy and reliability), 29 (bias and prejudice), 35–6 (gaps and contradictions), and 41 (eyewitnesses and hearsay evidence). It is also printed at the back of the book on page 125 as a convenient source of reference. When you use this master checklist ignore checkpoints which are irrelevant to the extract you are studying or for which you have insufficient information to make a sensible response.

Master Checklist — **Documentary Evidence**

1   What does the source tell you about the past?

2   What is the origin of the source? What type of evidence is it (e.g. diary, letter, newspaper report)? Is it likely to be reliable?

3   Why was the source written? Was it written to justify the writer's actions? Does the writer try to take credit for successes which other people claim for themselves? Does the writer put the blame for failures on to other people?

4   When was the source written? Is it a primary source dating from the time of the event which it describes? Or is it a secondary source?

5   Is there any clue or statement to show that it is an actual eyewitness account? Was the writer in a good position to say what happened? Does the source agree with other eyewitness accounts of the same event? Are there any reasons for thinking the eyewitness cannot be trusted entirely?

6   If the source was written years after the event is there any reason to doubt the accuracy of the writer's memory?

7   Which parts of the extract seem to you to be opinions and not facts which can be proved right or wrong? Are the opinions based on facts or on prejudice? Has the writer used words of approval or disapproval, or colourful or exaggerated phrases, to try to influence the reader?

8   Does the author show any other signs of bias or prejudice? Does the writer appear to take sides in an argument?

9   Are there any obvious mistakes or errors of fact in the extract? Which statements are supported by facts you know about from other sources? Does anything in the extract contradict other sources, or facts which you already know to be true?

10   Does the account give a distorted view of events which actually occurred? Has the author left out facts which tell a different story? Is any part of the extract an obvious lie or exaggeration? Are there any obvious gaps in the evidence, such as missing dates, facts or personalities?

Going through the Checklist

Here is an example of the way in which the master checklist can be used to evaluate a historical source. It describes a private meeting in Munich between the British prime minister, Neville Chamberlain, and the German dictator, Adolf Hitler, at the time of the signing of the Munich Agreement in 1938.

Hitler (centre) with his interpreter, Dr Paul Schmidt (left), and Neville Chamberlain (right) in September 1938

SOURCE A

Letter from Neville Chamberlain (British prime minister) to his two sisters: 2 October 1938

I asked Hitler about 1 in the morning [on 30 September], while we were waiting for the draftsmen, whether he would care to see me for another talk. He jumped at the idea, and asked me to come to his private flat, in a tenement house where the other floors are occupied by ordinary citizens. I had a very friendly and pleasant talk: on Spain (where he too said he had never had any territorial ambitions), economic relations with SE Europe, and disarmament. I did not mention colonies, nor did he. At the end I pulled out the declaration, which I had prepared beforehand, and asked if he would sign it. As the interpreter translated the words into German, Hitler frequently ejaculated '*Ja, Ja,*' and at the end he said 'yes, I will certainly sign it; when shall we do it?' I said 'Now', and we went at once to the writing-table, and put our signatures to the two copies which I had brought with me.

K. Feiling, *The Life of Neville Chamberlain*, Macmillan, 1946

1   *What does the source tell you about the past?*

It explains the circumstances which enabled Neville Chamberlain to get Hitler to sign the notorious document (Source B) which asserted 'the desire of our two peoples never to go to war with one another again'. On 1 October 1938 Chamberlain said of this document, 'I believe it is peace for our time.' Eleven months later he declared war on Germany.

2 *What is the origin of the source? What type of evidence is it (e.g. diary, letter, newspaper report)? Is it likely to be reliable?*

It is a private letter, from the British prime minister to his two sisters, giving a personal account of his private meeting with Hitler. At first sight it looks as if it must be the only authoritative source of information in English of what actually happened, since Hitler left no documents to confirm or deny Chamberlain's account of the meeting. However, there was someone else present at that meeting – 'the interpreter' who 'translated the words into German'. Hitler's interpreter was Dr Paul Schmidt and he later wrote his own account of this meeting (Source C). As you will see it does *not* confirm Chamberlain's impression of 'a very friendly and pleasant talk'.

3 *Why was the source written? Was it written to justify the writer's actions? Does the writer try to take credit for successes which other people claim for themselves? Does the writer put the blame for failures on to other people?*

It was undoubtedly written to justify the actions of the British prime minister, since they were, and still are, a matter of great controversy.

4 *When was the source written? Is it a primary source dating from the time of the event which it describes? Or is it a secondary source?*

It was written only two days after the event, so it is a primary source.

5 *Is there any clue or statement to show that it is an actual eyewitness account? Was the writer in a good position to say what happened?*

It is obviously an actual eyewitness account. The writer was in a good position to say what happened at the meeting. But he did not speak German fluently enough to speak directly to Hitler. Consequently the interpreter, who spoke both English and German, was in an even better position to say what happened (Source C).

6 *If the source was written years after the event is there any reason to doubt the accuracy of the writer's memory?*

This checkpoint does not apply since it was written only two days after the meeting.

7 *Which parts of the extract seem to you to be opinions and not facts which can be proved right or wrong?*

(a) That Hitler 'jumped at the idea' of signing the celebrated peace declaration.
(b) That Chamberlain and Hitler 'had a very friendly and pleasant talk'.

8 *Does the author show any other signs of bias or prejudice? Does the writer appear to take sides in an argument?*

No.

9 *Are there any obvious mistakes or errors of fact in the extract? Which statements are supported by facts you know about from other sources? Does anything in the extract contradict other sources or facts which you already know to be true?*

As you will see from Source C (below), the interpreter thought that Hitler looked 'pale and moody' and that he only 'listened absent-mindedly' to Chamberlain and contributed 'little to the conversation'. Nor did he agree that Hitler was keen to sign the declaration. 'My own feeling was that he agreed to the wording with a certain reluctance and I believe he appended his signature only to please Chamberlain.' [See Source C.] Bear in mind that these are differences *of opinion* and not differences *of fact.*

10 *Does the account give a distorted view of events which actually occurred?*

Not as far as we can tell from the extract on its own. But as you have just seen, Chamberlain took a much more optimistic view of Hitler's attitude than Hitler's own interpreter (who obviously knew him well) did (Source C).

SOURCE B

> We, the German Führer and Chancellor and the British Prime Minister, have had a further meeting today and are agreed in recognising that the question of Anglo-German relations is of the first importance for the two countries and for Europe.
>
> We regard the agreement signed last night and the Anglo-German Naval Agreement as symbolic of the desire of our two peoples never to go to war with one another again.
>
> We are resolved that the method of consultation shall be the method adopted to deal with any other questions that may concern our two countries, and we are determined to continue our efforts to remove possible sources of difference and thus to contribute to assure the peace of Europe.
>
> September 30. 1938.

The 'piece of paper' which Neville Chamberlain proudly displayed on his return to Britain after his meeting with Hitler

EXERCISES AND ACTIVITIES

SOURCE C

There was only a brief rest after the signing of the Agreement, for the next morning I was at Hitler's house to interpret the conversation with Chamberlain. Hitler looked quite different as he sat beside me, pale and moody. He listened absent-mindedly to Chamberlain's remarks about Anglo–German relations, disarmament and economic questions, contributing comparatively little to the conversation. Towards the end of the conversation Chamberlain drew the famous Anglo–German Declaration from his pocket . . . Slowly, emphasising each word, I translated this statement to Hitler.

I did not share Chamberlain's impression, expressed in a private letter of his now published, that Hitler eagerly assented to this declaration. My own feeling was that he agreed to the wording with a certain reluctance, and I believe he appended his signature only to please Chamberlain, without promising himself any too much from the effects of the declaration.

Dr Paul Schmidt, *Hitler's Interpreter*,
edited by R. H. C. Steed, Heinemann, 1951

1 *Use the checklist on page 54 to test this document. In particular take careful note of the balance between facts and opinions in this account of a very important meeting.*

2 *You probably have as much evidence as any historian can have of what happened at this private meeting between Hitler and Chamberlain. Write an account of this meeting using the facts which are common to both sources and explain the different ways in which the two participants (Chamberlain and Schmidt) describe Hitler's attitude to the meeting.*

3 *Read the following extracts (Sources D and E). For each Source go through the master checklist on page 54. What further light do they throw on the Munich Agreement? What do they tell you about British attitudes to Hitler in 1938?*

SOURCE D

'IT IS PEACE WITH HONOUR' SAYS CHAMBERLAIN

| Waving
The Pact |

Headlines in the Daily Herald *for Saturday 1 October 1938, describing the return of Neville Chamberlain from Munich*

BY HANNEN SWAFFER

DOWNING STREET, when the Premier reached home last evening, was crammed with a crowd that became hysterical.

A week before, boos and cries of "Save the Czechs" had been raised, when the Prime Minister returned after his second visit to Hitler.

Last evening, it was one wild frenzy of cheering. A newspaper seller, crying his wares, expressed it in a phrase. "Public Hero Number One," he shouted, although it was not on his poster.

SOURCE E

LETTERS IN THE *DAILY HERALD*, 1 OCTOBER 1938

We should have taken a firm line with Hitler from the beginning. It is plain to me that what held Hitler back from war was not Mussolini's intervention but fright at Britain's mobilisation.

The only hope for European peace is a real attempt at collective security, in which Russia must most emphatically be included.

Barbara Ayrton Gould

I consider that the settlement is only putting off the evil day. Czechoslovakia has gone as far as she possibly can, and Hitler's main object has not yet been expressed. Small countries abroad – I have just returned from Switzerland – are disappointed by the way Hitler is always allowed to be one step ahead.

Adelaide Livingstone (Director of Special Activities to the League of Nations Union)

NEWSPAPERS AND MAGAZINES

Newspapers have been published in Britain for over 300 years. They were first taxed in 1712 and this made newspapers costly to buy. In 1797, the government raised the newspaper tax, called Stamp Duty, much higher in order to make it too expensive for ordinary people to buy a newspaper. They did not want newspapers putting revolutionary ideas about freedom, justice and fair play into the heads of the masses. When Stamp Duty was abolished in 1855 it paved the way for cheap newspapers. But it was not until the end of the century, however, that the first really cheap newspapers were published for the millions of people who could now read – thanks to the improvements in state education in the late nineteenth century.

The first of the popular newspapers, the *Daily Mail*, cost a halfpenny [about 0.2p] when it was first published in 1896. Since then many other popular cheap newspapers have been published as well, including the *Daily Express* (1900), *Daily Mirror* (1904) and the *Sun* (1969). The first illustrated weekly magazines were begun in the 1840s with the founding of *The Illustrated London News* and the humorous weekly *Punch*. Many of these magazines and newspapers relied on advertisements so that they could be sold cheaply.

Old newspapers and magazines are an invaluable source of historical evidence. Some, such as *The Times*, have been copied on to microfilm.

The great advantage of newspapers and magazines as historical sources is that they were written at the time as contemporary news reports. So they are primary historical sources. They were also written for ordinary people to read, so they are often more interesting and easier to read than official documents. This is not to say that they are always to be trusted. Far from it.

Many news reports were based on hearsay evidence, on biased reports from prejudiced journalists, or even taken straight from the columns of other newspapers. There is often no way of knowing what has been left out of a report or how reliable the anonymous writer was. Opinions are sometimes quoted as if they were facts. Many newspapers were (and still are) biased in favour of a particular political party. Popular newspapers often distort or colour the facts in order to make a news story more interesting to the paper's readers.

KING AND PEOPLE IN THE STREETS OF LONDON, ARMISTICE DAY, NOVEMBER 11, 1918

Front page of The Sphere, *16 November 1918. What does this magazine cover tell you about the way in which Londoners greeted the ending of the First World War?*

EXERCISES AND ACTIVITIES

Look at these cuttings from three newspapers printed during the General Strike in May 1926.

1   *Go through each of these sources with the aid of the master checklist on page 54.*

2 *Which of these newspapers show political bias and in which direction? How do they try to convince their readers?*

3 *Compare the different ways in which all three newspapers appear to suggest that they know what the attitude of the general public was to the Strike.*

4 *Which newspaper would you have chosen to read had you wanted an unbiased account of the General Strike?*

SOURCE A

Daily Mail, *Wednesday*
5 May 1926

Yesterday the general strike came into force, showing that there is no extremity of violence from which the persons behind this conspiracy will shrink. Their ostensible leaders, the Parliamentary politicians - whose business it is to act the role of decoy ducks and win the support of the muddle-headed and simple - may deal in sobstuff about the "terrible situation", and their reluctance to go to extremes. But while they talk, their followers act. While lacrimose speeches, the House of Commons is treated to lacrimose speeches, the country is being "held up".

The British nation is eager to support its Government. It is waiting for its Government to act. It is looking to its Government to act. It is capable of any effort and of any sacrifice. But a nation cannot rally unless there is action; it cannot feel enthusiasm for a policy of sitting still. It never admired the policy of Kerensky, whose fault it was to imagine that words were the equivalent of deeds. When a fight is in progress (and the leaders of this strike have not hesitated to use the word "war") the only thing to do is to win it, not to think of what will happen if we do not win it. That is the policy which caused the failure of Jutland.

SOURCE B

The British Worker,
Monday 10 May 1926

NATION BEHIND THE T.U.C.

What a London Park Meeting Revealed

£55 COLLECTION

The quiet determination of the men on strike has impressed the outside public. The strikers' confidence and enthusiasm are contagious. They have spread to other sections of the nation.

"They don't look a bit like unemployed," remarked a young woman onlooker, who stood on the step of a West Norwood villa while a procession of transport strikers, be-medalled and in Sunday attire, marched in fours to Brockwell Park.

The immense crowd in the park gave a clear indication of where the sympathies of the British nation lie in this dispute. Many of the crowd were trade unionists, including strikers and their families, but at least a third of them were of the class which the Press loves to call "the general public" - bank and insurance clerks, small shopkeepers, holders of season-tickets, dwellers in suburban villas.

SOURCE C

The Daily Chronicle,
Thursday 13 May 1926

THE END OF THE GENERAL STRIKE.

QUESTIONS OF PRAISE AND BLAME.

Everybody's first thought to-day must be one of profound satisfaction that the general strike is over. The British people have come with credit out of a severe ordeal. During an unprecedented struggle, extending over nine days, not a cartridge—not even a blank cartridge—has been fired by a soldier, and no single fatal collision has occurred between the strikers and the civil power. There has been no food shortage, no panic, and wonderfully little loss of temper on either side. In a fair trial of strength, which we hope may never be repeated, the nation has stood up to the general strike and overcome it.

Trade unionists, we believe, will agree that the calling of the general strike was a serious blunder. It placed their movement in a false position. Mr. Lloyd George, in a message sent out early yesterday before the settlement, stated the matter in two sentences. "If," he said,

"The trade unions inflict a defeat on the Government, it will be an encouragement to the extreme elements in Labour to resort in future to the general strike as a weapon of offence, whenever they find their purpose thwarted by the normal working of democratic institutions. Such a defeat would sooner or later end the experiment of popular government in these islands."

The time will come later to review the situation fully, and to decide the respective responsibilities of the Government and the T.U.C., but some things are clear already. The Government committed a disastrous blunder, when on the night of Sunday, May 2, after its basis for continuing to treat with its miners had been actually accepted by the T.U.C., it abruptly banged the door on negotiations. But for that, it seems certain that a settlement would have been reached without a strike. There was nothing unusual in it being deferred to the final 24 hours; settlements very often are. What was unusual, was that, by the Government's folly, the final 24 hours were suddenly made unavailable for negotiation. Mr. Baldwin has never been a cheap Prime Minister, but this was one of his costliest mistakes.

JOURNALS, DIARIES AND LETTERS

Can you pick out any of the French words in this letter written by Napoleon Bonaparte? The date may confuse you. It reads 'Paris, le 20 fructidor au 8 de la République'. The French Revolutionaries had introduced a new calendar. Fructidor was the month of fruit (from 19 August to 22 September). As you can see, the letter was written in the 8th year of the Republic – 1800. So 'le 20 fructidor au 8 de la République' was actually 7 September 1800.

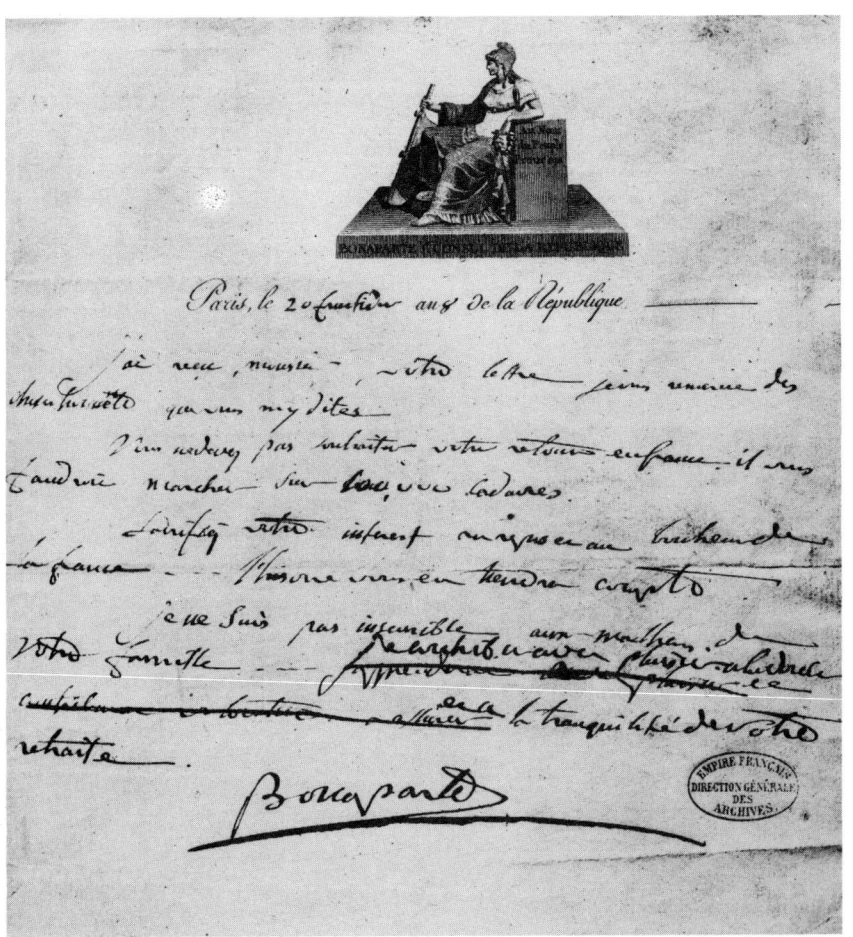

Travel journals, diaries and letters are an important source of historical evidence. This is because they are primary sources. The descriptions are usually eyewitness accounts. The writers often recall conversations which were still fresh in the mind when they wrote them. The more interesting personal diaries and journals have been published; the most famous is probably the *Diary of Samuel Pepys* written in the 1660s.

The diary entries you will see will probably fall into one of two main groups. The first group contains the many diaries which have been published primarily because the diarist is, or was, someone famous (such as Gladstone) or close to someone famous.

The second group contains diaries which have been published because they throw unusual or fascinating light on the past through the eyes of ordinary people with no particular claim to fame. These diaries are almost always interesting and provide a valuable source of information about everyday life in the past. For instance, the Reverend James Woodforde, the rector of a small Norfolk village near Norwich, wrote a well-known diary in the late eighteenth and early nineteenth centuries. His diary tells us about political events, such as 'The King of France Louis 16 inhumanely and unjustly beheaded on Monday last by his cruel, blood-thirsty subjects' (entry for Saturday 26 January 1793). It also tells us about everyday life – taxes, smuggling, and many other topics of interest in British history.

Collections of letters written by famous people, such as Queen Victoria, have also been published. These are particularly useful where the replies are published as well. Letters between politicians often help historians to discover the reasons why actions were taken in the past. It helps us to understand their motives.

For instance, Lord John Russell, the prime minister, wrote a letter to Prince Albert on 9 April 1848. In it he outlined the measures the government proposed to take against the Chartists, who were planning a huge demonstration (one man – one vote) for the following day. The Duke of Wellington, victor at Waterloo, had been called in to take control. 'The Military' were to be called out in the event of trouble. The Prince was assured that the prime minister had 'no doubt of their easy triumph over a London mob'.

Prince Albert began his reply by comparing the Chartists to 'evil-disposed people'. He did not doubt that the Military could deal with the situation and that 'the force of the law, the Government, and the good sense of the country' would prevail. But then he went on to point out that 'the number of workmen of all trades out of employment is very large' and that the problem had been increased by government cuts in public expenditure.

> Surely this is not the moment for the tax-payers to economise upon the working classes! . . . I think the Government is bound to do what it can to help the working classes over the present moment of distress.

At first glance journals, diaries and letters seem to be an ideal historical source. Those by famous people are often especially interesting where they tell us why certain actions were taken, and what the writer thought as well as what the writer did. But there are a number of drawbacks. Famous people know that their letters and diaries will probably be published for everyone to read. This is why they are often written as if the writer is attempting to justify or excuse certain actions. It is difficult to be certain that the writer is being honest. The diaries of ordinary people are often more revealing. Samuel Pepys tells us far more in his diary than he told people to their faces.

EXERCISES AND ACTIVITIES

Go through the master checklist on page 54 for each of these three sources in turn.

Mr Gladstone addressing the crowd from the balcony of Lord Rosebery's house in George Street, Edinburgh. The Graphic, April 1880.

SOURCE A

March 31. 1880

Gentlemen,

It has not been in my power to visit you individually; but you will agree with me that this contest is essentially patriotic, and is lifted far above the level of any question of personal attentions.

At home, in uphold diligent and careful legislation against neglect; economy and prudence against financial disorder; careful regard for the Constitution against invasion of the rights of Parliament: and abroad, not, as is absurdly alleged, a rule of inaction, but sympathy with freedom, and strict observance of justice and of honour, as the most vital of all British interests.

Before you read these lines, my name may have headed the poll in the great town of Leeds. But, however great the honour, it is unsought by me. My position will remain unaltered, and my regard and desire solely directed to the suffrages of Midlothian.

Part of a letter from Mr Gladstone to the electors of Midlothian dated 31 March 1880

SOURCE B

ENTRY FROM MR GLADSTONE'S DIARY, 5 APRIL 1880

Drove into Edinburgh about four. At 7.20 Mr Reid brought the figures of the poll – Gladstone 1579; Dalkeith 1368; quite satisfactory. Soon after 15 000 people being gathered in George Street, I spoke very shortly from the windows, and Rosebery followed, excellently well. Home about 10.

1   Copy out Gladstone's letter. Can you read every word? What did Gladstone think was the most important thing about the 1880 General Election?

2   What criticisms did he make of the Conservative government led by Lord Beaconsfield (formerly Benjamin Disraeli)? How did a Liberal Government led by Gladstone propose to deal with these issues?

3   Why did he begin his election address with the single word 'Gentlemen'?

4   Only 1579 people voted for him (out of a total poll of 2947 voters). Yet 15 000 people crowded into George Street to hear him speak. What does this tell you about the electoral system in 1880?

The third source (below) is taken from a diary which was written between 1899 and 1900 but was not discovered until seventy years later. It was written by Solomon Tshekisho Plaatje. He was a black South African who later went on to become an important writer and political leader. In 1912 he became the first secretary of the South African National Congress, the forerunner of the African National Congress. He was a member of the Barolong people, had been educated at Mission schools, and could write in Dutch and English as well as in South African languages, such as Xhosa, Tswana and Zulu. His diary is of great historical interest because he was living in Mafeking at the time of the famous siege during the Boer War.

SOURCE C

Wednesday 24th January 1900
There is a proclamation by the Colonel R. S. S. Baden-Powell that no food stores of any kind would in the future be sold to the public; and white people are now going to buy food in rations and be compelled to buy small quantities, the same as blacks. I have often heard the black folk say money is useless as you cannot eat it when you feel hungry, and now I have lived it and experienced it. The thing appears to be going from bad to worse. The big gun is still hammering away at us. It was particularly cruel today. One of its shells hit on the Market Square this morning. It bumped right up in the air and singled out old Moshuchwe's hut (one-and-a-half miles away): after its decline it entered the hut from the back, decapitating two women and wounding three brothers severely and one not dangerously. The old boy was not there.

The Boer War Diary of Sol T. Plaatje,
edited by John L. Comaroff, Macmillan, 1973

NB The full ration of food was 2s [10p] for a European man; 1s [5p] for a European woman; and 6d [2.5p] for a European child under 14 years. The full ration of food for a Black African man was 6d [2.5p].

5   *How did the siege of Mafeking directly affect the people who lived there?*

6   *How does this diary entry show that Black Africans were regarded as second class citizens?*

7   *How many people lived in Moshuchwe's hut?*

8   *How did 'the Colonel' become known the world over some years after the siege at Mafeking?*

MEMOIRS AND ORAL HISTORY

Oral history is spoken history. It is recollections about the past which are told to a historian rather than written down as memoirs. Oral history is usually first recorded on cassette, tape or video but may be written down at a later date. Oral historians record the reminiscences of ordinary people rather than those of the famous. They include the former coal miner talking about the General Strike in 1926 and the suffragette describing life in prison. Everyone has listened to oral history like this, even if it is only a grandparent talking about the 1930s or parents describing their own schooldays.

Nowadays historians recognise that oral history can make a big contribution to our understanding of the past. It is also a method of writing history which is open to anyone who has a cassette recorder.

Memoirs, on the other hand, are usually written by people of importance, such as a former prime minister or an admiral. The main difference compared with oral history is that they are written down instead of being spoken. They are almost always backed up in detail by documentary evidence, such as diaries, letters and official documents.

Both types of recollection – the spoken history and the written memoir – may be inaccurate and unreliable historical sources. This is because they depend heavily on human memory, which may or may not be faulty. Older people often tend to remember the past as being either much better or much worse than the present. Only rarely do they seem to think of it as being the same! If people were poor, they were much poorer than today. If they were happy, they were much happier than today! Not surprisingly, people recalling past events tend to justify their own actions. Writers of memoirs may skip over their mistakes and omit the less successful or more shameful periods of their lives. Above all, beware of the razor-sharp recollection of events which happened fifty or sixty years ago. This is not eyewitness evidence you can always trust.

EXERCISES AND ACTIVITIES

Use a cassette recorder to make an oral history which you can use when you study a topic in British and European history, such as the General Strike in 1926, the Abdication Crisis of 1936, evacuation during the Second World War, the Blitz, the referendum on Britain's entry into the European Economic Community in 1975, or the miners' strike of 1984–5. When you have made the tape recording treat it as documentary evidence and use the master checklist on page 54 to test the reliability of your historical sources.

USING PROPAGANDA AND ADVERTS

Nazi propaganda against the Jews. Young children shown reading Der Stürmer, a viciously anti-Jewish newspaper edited by the notorious Julius Streicher. How have the Jewish people been depicted here?

Propaganda is anything which deliberately sets out to persuade you to accept only one particular viewpoint, attitude or set of facts, irrespective of the truth. At its worst it is a campaign by ruthless people, such as the Nazis, to distort the truth in order to win backing for a war or a campaign of persecution. At its best, it is an effective advertisement designed to persuade people to give up a habit, such as cigarette smoking, which experts believe could damage their health. Nowadays television is the most powerful medium through which to advertise or disseminate propaganda. The Nazi Minister for Propaganda, Dr Josef Goebbels, recognised the power of broadcasting in the 1930s, long before it was effectively used in Britain or America.

'All Germany hears the Führer with the People's Radio'

Propaganda and advertisements can be useful historical sources in British and European history. Sometimes they throw light on people's attitudes and worries. Election posters tell us how political parties tried to discredit the policies of their opponents on subjects such as taxation or free trade.

EXERCISES AND ACTIVITIES

1   *Who is the 'Grand Old Magician' opposite? What was his Irish policy? What was the 'wonderful remedy'? Who are the three men (i.e. with the monocle, the long beard, and the distinctive moustache) sitting on the front row of the 'Theatre Royal Westminster'? What was the 'Great Liberal Cabinet Trick'?*

THE GRAND OLD MAGICIAN'S IRISH POLICY.

Advertisement for Beecham's Pills in The Illustrated London News, *24 April 1886*

A WONDERFUL REMEDY
GREAT IRISH PROBLEM
BEECHAM'S PILLS.

No settlement of any question, great or small, can be equitable and permanent which is not approached by all concerned in a perfectly unprejudiced spirit; no person who is in any way affected in health can be long in a truly unbiassed and judicial frame of mind; there-fore to secure a lasting and satisfactory settlement of the whole English-speaking race should be able to bring the full powers of the mind to bear upon the subject, un-trammelled by any disease or ill-humours of the body. To gain this end there is no better means than which are well known to carry off all the gross humours and impurities of the system, and thus, by sweeping and garnishing the temple of the soul, set the mind free to bring all its powers to bear on this, the most momentous question of modern times. Sold everywhere, in Boxes, 1s 1½d and 2s 9d.

Advertisement in December 1914 aimed at people wealthy enough to employ servants

5 Questions to those who employ male servants

1. HAVE you a Butler, Groom, Chauffeur, Gardener, or Gamekeeper serving you who, at this moment should be serving your King and Country?

2. Have you a man serving at your table who should be serving a gun?

3. Have you a man digging your garden who should be digging trenches?

4. Have you a man driving your car who should be driving a transport wagon?

5. Have you a man preserving your game who should be helping to preserve your Country?

A great responsibility rests on you. Will you sacrifice your personal convenience for your Country's need?

Ask your men to enlist TO-DAY.

The address of the nearest Recruiting Office can be obtained at any Post Office.

God Save the King.

2 *What does this advertisement tell you about Britain in 1914? Who was being asked to make a sacrifice?*

3   *How does this famous 'Wanted' poster make its point? Why do you think it was published? Does it tell us anything about the causes of the Second World War?*

WANTED!

FOR MURDER . . . FOR KIDNAPPING . . . FOR THEFT AND FOR ARSON

Can be recognised full face by habitual scowl. Rarely smiles Talks rapidly, and when angered screams like a child.

ADOLF HITLER

ALIAS

Adolf Schicklegruber, Adolf Hittler or Hidler

Last heard of in Berlin, September 3, 1939. Aged fifty, height 5ft. 8½in., dark hair, frequently brushes one lock over left forehead. Blue eyes. Sallow complexion, stout build, weighs about 11st. 3lb. Suffering from acute monomania, with periodic fits of melancholia. Frequently bursts into tears when crossed. Harsh, guttural voice, and has a habit of raising right hand to shoulder level. **DANGEROUS !**

Profile from a recent photograph. Black moustache. Jowl inclines to fatness. Wide nostrils. Deep-set, menacing eyes.

FOR MURDER   Wanted for the murder of over a thousand of his fellow countrymen on the night of the Blood Bath, June 30, 1934. Wanted for the murder of countless political opponents in concentration camps.

He is indicted for the murder of Jews, Germans, Austrians, Czechs, Spaniards and Poles. He is now urgently wanted for homicide against citizens of the British Empire.

Hitler is a gunman who shoots to kill. He acts first and talks afterwards.

No appeals to sentiment can move him. This gangster, surrounded by armed hoodlums, is a natural killer. The reward for his apprehension, dead or alive, is the peace of mankind.

FOR KIDNAPPING   Wanted for the kidnapping of Dr. Kurt Schuschnigg, late Chancellor of Austria. Wanted for the kidnapping of Pastor Niemoller, a heroic martyr who was not afraid to put God before Hitler. Wanted for the attempted kidnapping of Dr. Benes, late President of Czechoslovakia. The kidnapping tendencies of this established criminal are marked and violent. The symptoms before an attempt are threats, blackmail and ultimatums. He offers his victims the alternatives of complete surrender or timeless incarceration in the horrors of concentration camps.

FOR THEFT   Wanted for the larceny of eighty millions of Czech gold in March, 1939. Wanted for the armed robbery of material resources of the Czech State. Wanted for the stealing of Memelland. Wanted for robbing mankind of peace, of humanity, and for the attempted assault on civilisation itself. This dangerous lunatic masks his raids by spurious appeals to honour, to patriotism and to duty. At the moment when his protestations of peace and friendship are at their most vehement, he is most likely to commit his smash and grab.

His tactics are known and easily recognised. But Europe has already been wrecked and plundered by the depredations of this armed thug who smashes in without scruple.

FOR ARSON   Wanted as the incendiary who started the Reichstag fire on the night of February 27, 1933. This crime was the key point, and the starting signal for a series of outrages and brutalities that are unsurpassed in the records of criminal degenerates. As a direct and immediate result of this calculated act of arson, an innocent dupe, Van der Lubbe, was murdered in cold blood. But as an indirect outcome of this carefully-planned offence, Europe itself is ablaze. The fires that this man has kindled cannot be extinguished until he himself is apprehended—dead or alive !

THIS RECKLESS CRIMINAL IS WANTED—DEAD OR ALIVE!

Propaganda page in the Daily Mirror *published on the day after the outbreak of war in September 1939*

The political posters you can see below were used by the Liberal party before the 1906 General Election to attack the policies of the Conservative party led by A. (Arthur) J. Balfour, the prime minister, and the Tariff Reform League, led by Joseph Chamberlain. Chamberlain (who wore a monocle) was a former minister who had resigned from the government. The Tariff Reform League wanted to protect British farmers and manufacturers against the threat to their livelihoods from cheap foreign imports, such as corn and meat. At that time Britain had a policy of free trade. This meant that foreign producers did not have to pay customs duties on the goods they exported to Britain.

4 *How did the Liberals attempt to persuade electors that Tariff Reform would be bad for their pockets? What did they think of Conservative promises in the past?*

Reproduced in The Illustrated London News, 6 January 1906

Reproduced in The Illustrated London News, 6 January 1906

EVIDENCE FROM FICTION

Fiction simply means anything which has been invented or made up. Fiction can take many different forms. It includes stories, plays, novels, poems, ballads, rhymes and the words to songs.

Fiction is often based on fact: Authors often base their writings on things they have seen themselves in real life. There is little point in trying to get readers involved in the plot of a story if the descriptions of politicians, ordinary people, houses, shops, working conditions and clothes of the characters do not ring true as well. The stories are fictional but the way of life described is usually typical of its time. This can be confirmed by comparing written accounts in novels and stories with factual descriptions, photographs and pictures.

Fiction also throws light on the way in which people behaved, such as their manners and their customs. It can help us to understand how people spoke and their attitudes to servants or to employers. Descriptions of political events, such as strikes and election meetings, are often particularly vivid because they are written by excellent writers who knew how to make a scene come to life. This is why fiction can be a useful source of historical evidence when studying British history. Foreign fiction (in translation) can be equally useful as a source when studying European history.

Like most historical sources, however, there are drawbacks. If a writer, such as Charles Dickens, felt strongly about an injustice he often exaggerated the problem, or based his story on a particularly bad case (such as the schoolmaster Wackford Squeers in *Nicholas Nickleby*). There is a danger that the writer of fiction may make a particular situation appear to be much worse, or much better, in fiction than it really was in fact.

Going through the Checklist

You can apply the same checks to fiction as you would to a factual historical source. (Use the master checklist on page 54.) This extract comes from the short story *Boule de Suif*. It was written by Guy de Maupassant about ten years after the end of the Franco-Prussian War.

> For several days in succession remnants of a defeated army had been passing through the town. They were not disciplined units, but hordes of stragglers. The men were unshaven and unwashed, their uniforms were in rags and they slouched along without colours or orders. . . . People said that the Prussians would soon be in Rouen . . .

And now a deep calm, a dumb terrified foreboding had settled down upon the city... Life seemed to have stopped; the shops were closed and the streets deserted. Sometimes one of the townspeople, terrified by the silence, slunk along keeping close to the walls.

The agony of waiting made everyone long for the arrival of the enemy. On the afternoon of the day following the departure of the French troops, a few uhlans, suddenly appearing from nowhere, rode rapidly through the town. A little later... the German army began to arrive, the cobble-stones ringing under the heavy rhythmical tread of the marching battalions.

Guy de Maupassant, *Boule de Suif*,
translated by H. N. P. Sloman, Penguin, 1946

Prussian uhlans (lancers) entering a French town. The Graphic, 17 September 1870.

1 *What does the source tell you about the past?*

It describes the way in which Rouen was abandoned by the French army and then occupied by advancing German troops during the Franco–Prussian War.

2 *What is the origin of the source? What type of evidence is it? Is it likely to be reliable?*

It is a short story. The author, Guy de Maupassant, was educated in Rouen and served in the army during the Franco–Prussian War.

3 *Why was the source written?*

As a short story to entertain his readers.

4 *When was the source written? Is it a primary source dating from the time of the event which it describes? Or is it a secondary source?*

It was written in about 1880 and is, therefore, a primary source written shortly after the Franco–Prussian War. Nonetheless, it is still a work of fiction and not of fact.

Checkpoints 5, 6, 7 and 8 do not apply since the story was written as fiction and not as a factual account of events.

9 *Are there any obvious mistakes or errors of fact in the extract? Which statements are supported by facts you know about from other sources? Does anything in the extract contradict other sources or facts which you already know to be true?*

See checkpoint 10.

10 *Does the account give a distorted view of events which actually occurred? Has the author left out facts which tell a different story?*

In most cases checkpoints 9 and 10 would not apply, either, since *Boule de Suif* is a work of fiction. But Maupassant sets his story in Rouen, which the Prussians entered on 5 December 1870. *Cassell's History of the War* (dating from about 1872) claims that the Rouen authorities invited the Prussian troops into the city to quell a riot – 'The square of the Hôtel de Ville was in the hands of the mob.' This was later denied by the Municipal Council of Rouen, who claimed, instead, that 'At five o'clock [on 5 December 1870] General Briand told the Mayor that . . . he was giving orders to beat a retreat. . . . A few hours later when the enemy invaded . . . the Mayor could only say "You are here by force. The French troops left us this morning." '

EXERCISES AND ACTIVITIES

1   *Which parts of the extract from Maupassant's* Boule de Suif *may not be strictly accurate?*

The short extracts which follow come from the novel *The Pickwick Papers* by Charles Dickens, published in 1836. They describe an election at Eatanswill (Dickens based his description on the small Suffolk town of Sudbury).

'The Successful Candidate'. Cartoon drawn by Phiz for The Illustrated London News, 24 July 1852.

EXTRACT A

Large blue silk flags were flying from the windows of the Town Arms Inn and bills were posted in every sash, intimating, in gigantic letters, that the Honourable Samuel Slumkey's Committee sat there daily. A crowd of idlers were assembled in the road, looking at a hoarse man in the balcony, who was apparently talking himself very red in the face on Mr Slumkey's behalf; but the force and point of whose arguments were somewhat impaired by the perpetual beating of four large drums which Mr Fizkin's committee had stationed at the street corner.

EXTRACT B

'And what are the probabilities as to the result of the contest?' inquired Mr Pickwick.

'Why, doubtful, my dear sir; rather doubtful as yet,' replied the little man. 'Fizkin's people have got three-and-thirty voters in the lock-up coach-house at the White Hart.'

'In the coach-house!' said Mr Pickwick, considerably astonished by this second stroke of policy.

'They keep 'em locked up there till they want 'em,' resumed the little man. 'The effect of that is, you see, to prevent our getting at them; and even if we could, it would be no use, for they keep them very drunk on purpose. Smart fellow, Fizkin's agent – very smart fellow, indeed.'

EXTRACT C

'Nothing has been omitted, I hope?' said the Honourable Samuel Slumkey.

'Nothing has been left undone, my dear sir – nothing whatever. There are twenty washed men at the street door for you to shake hands with; and six children in arms that you're to pat on the head, and inquire the age of. Be particular about the children, my dear sir; it has always a great effect, that sort of thing.'

'I'll take care,' said the Honourable Samuel Slumkey.

'And perhaps my dear sir,' said the cautious little man, 'perhaps if you *could* – I don't mean to say it's indispensable – but if you *could* manage to kiss one of 'em, it would produce a very great impression on the crowd.'

2   *Go through the master checklist printed on page 54.*

3   *Who were the two candidates? Which parts of this account sound more like fiction than fact?*

4   *What do the extracts tell you about elections in the early nineteenth century?*

5   *How is a modern election similar to, and different from, the Eatanswill election?*

6   *What are the similarities between the scene depicted by Phiz and the one described by Dickens?*

FACTS FROM PICTURES

Engraving of a picture by William Hogarth showing John Wilkes, an eighteenth-century reformer and political agitator. Do you think Hogarth approved of Wilkes?

Pictures created shortly after an event are called *contemporary pictures*. Historians often use them as primary sources. They include paintings, sketches, cartoons, drawings, engravings, pictures on pottery, pictures on stamps, pictures on song sheets, statues, carvings, etc.

Many artists have used their pictures to say something about the society in which they live. The wealth of detail in Hogarth's pictures makes them one of the most important sources of information we have about British history in the early eighteenth century.

The main drawback to the use of contemporary pictures is that we cannot always be certain that the picture created by the artist actually portrays real things. The concern of many artists in the past was to produce a pleasing picture which was well composed and well drawn or painted. The artist who drew a battle scene often did so from the point of view of one of the participating armies. Artists have the freedom to emphasize the good or bad points in a scene. Two illustrators depicting the same scene or event can sometimes produce two very different pictures. This is demonstrated in the illustrations on this page. Both depict the same event – the launching of a new lifeboat at Blackpool in 1885.

The Illustrated London News, *10 October 1885*

The Graphic, *10 October 1885. How does this picture differ from the illustration printed in* The Illustrated News? *What are the main similarities?*

We cannot always be certain that the pictures we see were actually drawn or painted on the spot or even that they were based on sketches made in the field. Some illustrations were drawn from photographs, or based on newspaper reports and eyewitness accounts. Many detailed and lifelike pictures were 'imagined' by the artist in a studio. As a consequence we cannot always be sure that realistic pictures of people, places and events are the eyewitness primary sources they may at first appear to suggest (such as the pictures of the Charge of the Light Brigade on pages 44 and 45).

'View of the Conflagration of the City of Hamburgh', The Illustrated London News, 14 May 1842

Even a picture accompanying a news item in an illustrated news magazine or newspaper could have been drawn in the studio rather than at the scene of the event. When the first issue of *The Illustrated London News* was published in 1842 it carried a news report and picture of a great fire in Hamburg in Germany. But the artist had not been to Hamburg! Instead, he copied an old picture of the city, made flames come out of the buildings, and drew in figures of people to show the crowds.

A further drawback is that in many cases you will not be able to find out much about the origins of the contemporary pictures you see. This is partly because many pictures were drawn by anonymous or unknown artists and partly because pictures are often reproduced in books without giving an indication of their actual origin.

Political cartoons based on recent events are another important source of information used by historians studying British and European history. They often sum up a controversy, crisis or great event in a sketch and a short caption, such as the celebrated cartoon which John Leech drew when Czar Nicholas I died on 2 March 1855. Russia had suffered a defeat on 17 February at the battle of Eupatoria in the Crimean War. Earlier the Czar had claimed that the Russian winter always came to the aid of a Russian army – 'Russia has two generals in whom she can confide – Generals Janvier [January] and Février [February].'

What was the point of this cartoon?

"GENERAL FÉVRIER" TURNED TRAITOR.

Checklist — **Pictures from the Past**

You will not always be able to answer every checkpoint in this list when you study a picture. This is because most pictures are printed without giving full details of when, where, why, and how they were produced, and by whom.

You can see how each of these checkpoints applies to the pictures that follow on pages 81–3.

1   *Does the picture attempt to portray realistically people, events, buildings, etc., or does it poke fun at them by means of a cartoon or an exaggerated drawing (called a caricature)?*

2   *What does the picture show? What does it tell us about the past?*

3   *When was the picture drawn? Was it drawn at roughly the same time as the event or feature it depicts? Is it a primary source? If no date is given can you estimate roughly the date when it was drawn from the clothes worn by the people in the picture, from the styles of vehicles (such as motor cars), or from other clues?*

4   *Why was the picture drawn or painted? Was it simply an illustration (e.g. to accompany a news item or to illustrate a book) or is there any reason to think the artist was using the picture to make you feel in a certain way about the events or people depicted? For instance, was it drawn or painted to make you want to protest against an injustice, or to feel excited, or sad, or nostalgic for an old way of life, or patriotic, or self-satisfied, or envious of someone else's way of life?*

5   *Does the picture show something which could not be shown in any other way, such as the interior of a courtroom where photographs are not permitted?*

6   *Even if it looks like a realistic picture is there any reason to think it is a product of the artist's imagination rather than a portrayal of an actual scene or event?*

7   *If the picture is a cartoon what was the artist getting at? What does the cartoon tell you about the topic, events or people portrayed? What does it tell you about the attitude of the artist who drew the cartoon or of the magazine which published it?*

'Guards Passing Over Vauxhall Bridge' appeared in The Illustrated London News on 19 July 1856. Even if we did not know the exact date we could guess that it dates from the period of the Crimean War just by looking at the very distinctive crinolines worn by the women and girls in the foreground.

This realistic picture of the Charge of the Light Brigade (see pages 41–8) appeared in The Illustrated London News on 23 December 1854. It is an artist's impression of what the battle looked like to the participants. But since the cavalry are shown charging towards the artist, it could only have been drawn by a Russian artist about to be cut down by a Hussar's sabre! Compare it with the two other pictures of the Charge of the Light Brigade on pages 44 and 45.

Scene on London's embankment showing stockbrokers returning home in the rush hour. See if you can estimate roughly the date when this picture was drawn. What does it tell you about London at that time? Why do you think the artist drew the picture? What did he want you to feel?

Drawing of Christabel Pankhurst in court, The Sphere, *31 October 1908*

THE THREE EMPERORS

This cartoon, drawn by Sir John Tenniel, appeared in Punch on 20 September 1884. It shows Prince Bismarck as the power behind the formation of the Dreikaiserbund – the League (bund) of Three (Drei) Emperors (kaiser) – the Emperors of Germany, Austria and Russia. How did Tenniel show what he thought about the part played by Prince Bismarck in the formation of this alliance?

Going through the Checklist

SOURCE A

Punch, 15 April 1848

"NOT SO *VERY* UNREASONABLE!!! EH?"

1 *Does the picture attempt to portray realistically people, events, buildings, etc., or does it poke fun at them by means of a cartoon or an exaggerated drawing (called a caricature)?*

It is a cartoon from *Punch*.

2 *What does the picture show? What does it tell us about the past?*

It shows a working man (a Chartist) delivering the Charter to the prime minister in 1848. The Charter was a massive petition containing millions of signatures of people, most of them from the working class. They were demanding voting rights, such as one man, one vote.

3 *When was the picture drawn? Was it drawn at roughly the same time as the event or feature it depicts? Is it a primary source?*

This is a primary source since it was published on 15 April 1848.

4 *Why was the picture drawn or painted?*

It was drawn at the time of a great Chartist meeting in London which the government feared might lead to a serious riot, if not a rebellion. To counter any such danger they put the Duke of Wellington in charge of the police and army in the city (see page 63).

Checkpoints 5 and 6 do not apply.

7 *If the picture is a cartoon what was the artist getting at? What does the cartoon tell you about the events or the people portrayed? What does it tell you about the attitude of the artist who drew the cartoon or of the magazine which published it?*

The artist says that the demands of the Chartists were not so very unreasonable after all and that the fears of the government were unfounded.

SOURCE B

The Russian Duma in session in 1906. Drawn by a French artist, Louis Remy Sabattier. The Illustrated London News, 30 June 1906.

1 *Does the picture attempt to portray realistically people, events, buildings, etc., or does it poke fun at them by means of a cartoon or an exaggerated drawing (called a caricature)?*

It is a fairly realistic drawing.

2 *What does the picture show? What does it tell us about the past?*

It depicts the newly-elected Russian Parliament, the Duma, in 1906 after the revolutionary movements of 1905 had forced the Czar to make some limited reforms. In fact, the members of the Duma were only elected by a small percentage of the Russian people. They had little real power.

3 *When was the picture drawn? Was it drawn at roughly the same time as the event or feature it depicts? Is it a primary source?*

It was drawn in 1906 at the time of the event depicted. It is therefore a primary historical source.

4 *Why was the picture drawn or painted?*

Presumably because it was thought that people in Europe might be interested to see Russia's first steps towards democracy.

5 *Does the picture show something which could not be shown in any other way?*

Yes. *The Illustrated London News* claimed that Sabattier was 'the only artist who has been permitted to make sketches of the Duma in session'. Photography was forbidden.

6 *Even if it looks like a realistic picture is there any reason to think it is a product of the artist's imagination rather than a portrayal of an actual scene or event?*

No.

SOURCE C

An Irish eviction, The Illustrated London News, 15 January 1887

1 *Does the picture attempt to portray realistically people, events, buildings, etc., or does it poke fun at them by means of a cartoon or an exaggerated drawing (called a caricature)?*

It is a very realistic picture, but obviously it has been carefully composed to make a strong and dramatic effect.

2 *What does the picture show? What does it tell us about the past?*

It shows the eviction of an old man, a woman and baby, and a small girl from a cottage in County Kerry during the Irish Troubles of the late 1880s. It highlights the harsh use the British government made of troops and police to enforce the rights of the landlords against their tenants in Ireland.

3 *When was the picture drawn? Was it drawn at roughly the same time as the event or feature it depicts? Is it a primary source?*

It is a primary source drawn in 1886 or 1887.

4 *Why was the picture drawn or painted? Was it simply an illustration (e.g. to accompany a news item or to illustrate a book) or is there any reason to think the artist was using the picture to make you feel in a certain way about the events or people depicted?*

The picture illustrated a news item about evictions in Ireland. Most people sympathised with the evicted tenants rather than with the landlords. This is why the look in the old man's eyes was drawn to excite sympathy. So, too, was the plight of the young grandchildren and their mother.

6 *Even if it looks like a realistic picture is there any reason to think it is a product of the artist's imagination rather than a portrayal of an actual scene or event?*

The dramatic nature of the illustration suggests that the artist may have used his imagination. Although it was drawn by A. Forestier (you can see his name in the bottom lefthand corner) the caption in *The Illustrated London News* says that it is 'From a sketch by our special artist'. In other words Forestier drew this picture in his English studio from a sketch supplied by another artist in Ireland!

Checkpoints 5 and 7 do not apply.

EXERCISES AND ACTIVITIES

Go through the checkpoints on page 80 with each of the illustrations shown below and on page 88.

Liberty Leading the People *(Louvre Museum, Paris). This painting by Eugène Delacroix shows the revolutionaries defending a bridge in the centre of Paris during the 1830 French Revolution.*

Russian cartoon drawn in 1906. Does this cartoon tell you more about the Duma than the picture printed on page 85?

Engraving showing the expulsion of a group of Jews from eastern Europe. The Illustrated London News, 14 November 1885. The text accompanying the picture explained that the Jews of eastern Europe were frequently subjected to persecution by mobs and were insufficiently protected by the law or by the police.

FACTS FROM PHOTOGRAPHS

Street scene in Kelvedon in Essex in the middle of the nineteenth century

Look at this photograph. Here recorded for all time are just a few seconds of a sunny summer's day sometime in the early 1850s. At this time there were public executions in Britain; Africa was still largely unexplored; Queen Victoria was a young woman in her early thirties; it was not yet compulsory to go to school.

Nearly 140 years have passed since then. Yet you can still capture the excitement of these villagers in Kelvedon in Essex. Perhaps some of them were seeing a camera for the very first time. It is not hard to imagine the photographer who took the photograph – buried inside a deep black cape, focusing the huge box-like camera mounted on a heavy tripod in the middle of the road. Traffic was not a problem on country roads in those days!

When we look at a photograph like this we are like eyewitnesses. It is true we do not see the picture in colour. Nor do we see the movement in the scene. But there are clues in the photograph which we can use to find out more about the scene it portrays.

Notice how the people in the photograph are all facing the camera. Notice, too, that the horses are blurred. This is because it took several seconds to take a photograph with the earliest cameras. Action photographs were not possible then. This is why most photographs were carefully posed. People took up positions they could hold for several seconds at a time. They knew they were being photographed.

Look at the short shadows on the ground. The photograph could not have been taken in winter. Shadows like these help you to judge the season of the year when a photograph was taken. Photographers had to take their photographs when the sun was at its height – at midday. In Britain shadows as short as this are thrown by the sun only at midday in summer. Yet everyone is wearing heavy clothes!

We have no precise date for this photograph but there is a clue which tells us the photograph was taken in the period between about 1845 and 1860. Three of the men in the photograph are wearing distinctive tall hats, called stovepipe hats, which were only worn during this period.

Picture clues like these can help you to make better use of the photographs you see from the past. But bear in mind that although a photograph can give you the impression of being an eyewitness, it is far from certain that what it shows is a fair representation of reality itself. Most photographers carefully select the best viewpoints for their photographs if they can. They decide what the photograph will show, *not* the camera! This photograph may or may not be typical of Kelvedon. It may or may not be typical of a Victorian village in about 1850. Questions like these can only be answered by studying other photographs and comparing them with pictures and written accounts.

Bear in mind, too, that the camera can also lie. Photographs are sometimes altered to improve the appearance of the people shown in the pictures or to block out something which spoils the view. Some photographs have even been deliberately faked.

This photograph, showing the immense size of the R34 airship, was printed in The Graphic *on 12 July 1919. How do you think the photograph was taken?*

The first cameras were very heavy and cumbersome. They were also expensive and, as you have seen, recorded anything that moved as a blur on the photograph. Photographers needed good sunlight to take good photographs. This is one reason why it is difficult to find photographs of Victorian slums which match the appalling conditions described by writers such as Henry Mayhew or Charles Dickens. The slums were dark and gloomy. They were crowded with people. They were also dangerous places for the wealthy to set up their expensive cameras! It was only the invention of the Kodak camera using rollfilm in 1889 and the development of fast shutter speeds which enabled photographers to take candid (unposed) photographs without being observed.

Checklist — **Photographs**

1   *What does the photograph show? What does it tell us about the past?*

2   *When and where was the photograph taken? If no date is given use clues to estimate the date.*

3   *Why was the photograph taken? Is there any reason to think the photographer chose a viewpoint or a subject to make us feel in a certain way about the event or people depicted?*

4   *Is there any sign that the people in the photograph are posing for the photographer? Were they aware of the camera? Does this make any difference to the value of the photograph?*

5   *Is there any reason to think that the photograph is not a typical example of what it appears to show? Is there any reason to think that it may have been altered in any way?*

Going through the Checklist

The battle of Sedan, Franco–Prussian War, 1–2 September 1870

1   *What does the photograph show? What does it tell us about the past?*

This unusual action photograph appears to show Prussian troops firing at the cameraman during the battle of Sedan. We can see the position of the Prussian forces in the field and along the road.

2 *When and where was the photograph taken? If no date is given, use clues to estimate the date.*

It was taken at the battle of Sedan, 1–2 September 1870.

3 *Why was the photograph taken? Is there any reason to think the photographer chose a viewpoint or a subject to make us feel in a certain way about the event or people depicted?*

It puts us in the alarming position of the eyewitness under fire on a battlefield.

4 *Is there any sign that the people in the photograph are posing for the photographer? Were they aware of the camera?*

It is difficult to say. Many of the Prussians are looking straight at the photographer. They may have been told to stand still!

5 *Is there any reason to think that the photograph is not a typical example of what it appears to show?*

Since most of the soldiers could have been easily picked off by a French rifleman standing by the camera, it is fairly safe to assume that the Prussian soldiers did not feel they were in any particular danger! If so, then this is not the terrifying battlefield scene it first appeared to be!

EXERCISES AND ACTIVITIES

1 *Do you think the photograph of the battle of Sedan was posed? Or is it a genuine photograph of a battle in progress?*

Look at these two photographs in turn and go through the checklist printed on page 91.

Wives of Prussian officers making bandages during the short war with Austria in 1866. How could you estimate the approximate date from this photograph?

'On Guard! The Poilu Sentry in the Ruhr'. The Graphic, Saturday, 3 February 1923. French and Belgian soldiers marched into the Ruhr industrial area in January 1923 after Germany fell behind with the payment of compensation at the end of the First World War. [NB 'Poilu' was the name for a French infantryman.]

EVIDENCE IN SOUND AND ON FILM

The first sound recordings were made by Thomas Alva Edison in 1877. The first moving films were made in the 1890s. These two great inventions provided historians with important new sources of evidence. Since they are not in printed form, however, their value in the study of history has not always been appreciated. Only since the coming of television has effective use been made of old film for the benefit of the general public. As a result, people can now see movie film of the funeral of Queen Victoria in 1901 or watch the coronation of Queen Elizabeth II in 1953. Old movie films enable us to see or hear some of the events of history as they happened.

The main drawback to the use of movie film is that it can be easily *edited* (altered) to show whatever the film editor wants us to see. Lengths of movie film can be cut out and then stuck back together in a different order. It is very easy to assume that because the images are moving in a documentary film we are actually seeing events in sequence exactly as they happened at the time. In many cases you are but you cannot be certain of this! Movie film has been one of the most powerful weapons used by people involved in propaganda (as in Nazi Germany) and in advertising (see also pages 67–71).

On pages 25–7 you saw evidence relating to the death of Emily Wilding Davison after the Epsom Derby on 4 June 1913. A movie film was made of the race and shown at the Palace Theatre in London. This is how a journalist on *The Times* described the film when he saw it for the first time on Derby night, 1913.

The tragic incident at the 1913 Derby

A CINEMATOGRAPH VIEW

The scene at Tattenham Corner was shown on the cinematograph at the Palace Theatre last night. Viewed from a point opposite Tattenham Corner the vast crowd was seen with every head turned in the direction from which the horses were coming. A moment later a bunch, so closely packed that it is scarcely possible to distinguish one horse from another, passed at a great pace. There is a pause for a moment, and suddenly a woman is seen to spring forward from behind the white rails, but as she sets foot upon the course two horses come by. There is a flicker and a flash of white, the woman is prostrate on the turf and a jockey is flung head foremost from his mount and lies in a huddled heap a dozen yards from the woman. A moment more and the remaining horses have passed, but the jockey and the woman lie still and silent, and then the great crowd, moved by a common impulse, closes round them.

The Times, Thursday, 5 June 1913

As it happens, the clip of film described in this report has been included in at least one schools' broadcast.

To the eyewitnesses at Epsom, glued to the race, the incident, which was over in a flash, came as a complete shock. It was unthinkable that anyone would actually want to run on to the track during the race. Not surprisingly, they had different versions of what happened in the midst of the confusion.

The modern viewer of the movie film shown on a video recorder has no such excuse! Slow motion and the rewind button can be used to get an instant replay of history! In other words you can be an eyewitness to an important historical event, but with the added advantage of being able to repeat the film over and over again until you think you know for sure what happened.

Almost every historian who has ever described this event in print (including the author until he saw the video recording of a schools' broadcast!) is on record as saying that Emily Wilding Davison 'threw herself under the King's horse'. As you will recall (pages 25–7), the eye-witness at the Derby did not say this but everyone later assumed that this is what must have happened.

Here is a modern 'eyewitness' account of the 1913 Derby written after watching about a dozen replays of this incident on a video recorder.

> Emily Wilding Davison can be seen clearly ducking under the barrier after the leading horses have passed. She stands upright in the middle of the racecourse, facing the remaining horses in the race. Her arms appear to be stretched outwards. At no time does she fling herself under the hooves of a horse. She seems bewildered, at first, trying to grab at the reins of three horses which are close together and passing her far too quickly for her to have any chance of stopping them. Then there is a short gap in the field. It is enough to give her the chance to position herself and reach up to the next horse as it races towards her. She grabs at the reins again but is knocked down and the horse and the jockey also fall. Two other horses ride past as they lie on the ground.

In other words, the 'cinematograph film' proves conclusively that:

- Emily Wilding Davison did not throw herself under the hooves of the King's horse. Far from it. She was standing upright all the time and her only motion when the horse approached was to reach up with her hands towards the reins.
- It was sheer chance that the horse that knocked her down was Anmer, the King's horse. In fact, she tried to stop the earlier horses as soon as she stepped on to the race track.
- Anmer was third from last at Tattenham Corner. It was *not* leading the field, nor was it the last horse in the race. This corrects the statements in Sources A and D on page 25.

These may seem trivial points but they do have some importance to the history of the suffragette movement. In the first place they suggest that Emily Davison did not really set out to become a martyr at all, although she did want to stop or disrupt the race. In fact she gives every impression of having been taken aback by the speed of the horses. So perhaps she was not quite the heroine and martyr portrayed by the suffragettes in their subsequent literature. Equally she was not the 'half-demented' woman depicted by many commentators and historians both at the time and since.

EXERCISES AND ACTIVITIES

Look closely at clips of old newsreel film on a video recorder or whenever an old documentary film is shown on schools' television. Use your eyes and ears to note carefully what happens. Record your observations as an eyewitness would have done had he or she been a witness to the same event.

If possible take the opportunity to view the film of the 1913 Derby. Write your own 'eyewitness' account of the incident and compare it with those printed above on pages 94 and 95.

FACTS FROM STATISTICS

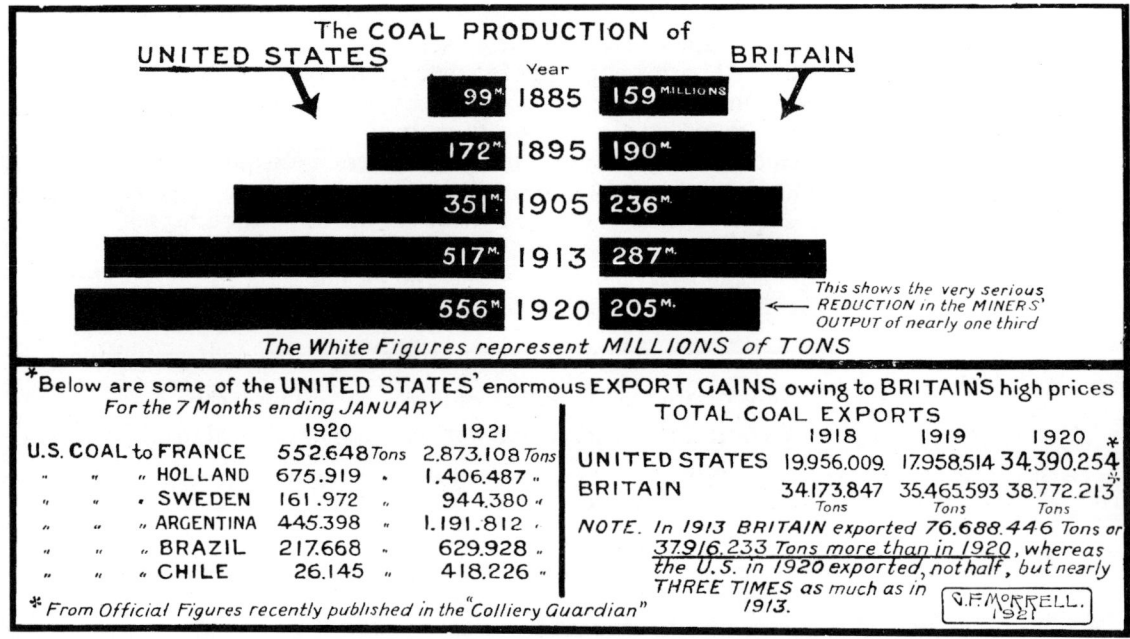

The COAL PRODUCTION of

UNITED STATES — Year — BRITAIN

	Year	
99ᴹ	1885	159 MILLIONS
172ᴹ	1895	190ᴹ
351ᴹ	1905	236ᴹ
517ᴹ	1913	287ᴹ
556ᴹ	1920	205ᴹ

← This shows the very serious REDUCTION in the MINER'S OUTPUT of nearly one third

The White Figures represent MILLIONS of TONS

*Below are some of the UNITED STATES' enormous EXPORT GAINS owing to BRITAIN'S high prices

For the 7 Months ending JANUARY

	1920	1921
U.S. COAL to FRANCE	552.648 Tons	2.873.108 Tons
" " " HOLLAND	675.919 "	1.406.487 "
" " • SWEDEN	161.972 "	944.380 "
" " " ARGENTINA	445.398 "	1.191.812 "
" " " BRAZIL	217.668 "	629.928 "
" " " CHILE	26.145 "	418.226 "

TOTAL COAL EXPORTS

	1918	1919	1920
UNITED STATES	19.956.009	17.958.514	34.390.254
BRITAIN	34.173.847	35.465.593	38.772.213
	Tons	Tons	Tons

NOTE. In 1913 BRITAIN exported 76.688.446 Tons or 37.916.233 Tons more than in 1920, whereas the U.S. in 1920 exported, not half, but nearly THREE TIMES as much as in 1913.

J.F.MORRELL. 1921

* From Official Figures recently published in the "Colliery Guardian"

Why do you think this graph and the statistics underneath were published in The Graphic *on 14 May 1921 at the time of a coalminers' strike? What were these statistics designed to show?*

Statistics are an important source of information for the historian. The most important sources of statistics in British history are the official census reports which have been published every ten years since the first Census in 1801. Official statistics of wartime casualties, army recruitment, agricultural and industrial production, length of railway line, numbers of people unemployed, and countless other statistics have also been published. Statistics like these are invaluable since they help us to measure the effect of war, the progress or decline of industries, and the growth or decline of towns.

But there are problems. Some statistics can be misleading. They may have been collected or counted in circumstances which led to inaccuracies. The first census reports were compiled from census returns, completed by householders, many of whom were illiterate. Sometimes the statistics are biased. They may also be incomplete.

Many printed statistics, like opinion polls, are based on samples, instead of being complete surveys. Statistics for 1800 tell us about 1800. These may or may not be typical of the 1800s as a whole. Statistics for London tell us about London, not about the rest of Britain. Unfortunately, you will rarely have the chance to check for yourself when, how, why, and where the statistics were collected and whether they are reliable.

This is why it is best to treat all statistics with a certain amount of caution and to use them as a guide rather than as proof. In particular, beware of believing statistics just because they back up your own or other people's arguments!

Checklist — **Statistics**

1 *When and how were the statistics collected? Who collected them? Were they in a position to collect accurate or reliable statistics? Can we be certain they are not guesses, estimates, approximations or even lies?*

2 *Is it likely that someone else working in exactly the same way would collect the same statistics? If not, why not?*

3 *Are the statistics complete or only a sample of all the possible statistics which could have been recorded?*

4 *Who selected the statistics for use and how were they chosen?*

5 *What do the statistics tell you about the past? What do they prove? If they are quoted to back up a statement do they really support the conclusions drawn from them by the writer?*

6 *Are the statistics used to support a statement which may be biased or prejudiced?*

7 *If averages are used, do they mean anything? See if you can find out how they were calculated.*

Going through the Checklist

Read this item from the January 1903 issue of *The Leisure Hour*, a popular family magazine of the 1900s.

> The German Admiralty publishes some striking information regarding the growth of the Kaiser's navy during the past twenty years. Roughly speaking the strength of the German navy within this short period has increased threefold.
>
> In 1881 the estimates provided for 11,352 men, in 1886 for 14,682, in 1891 for 17,083, in 1896 for 21,835, and in 1902 for 31,171. The following table shows the increase in the number of officers:

	1881	1891	1901
OFFICERS			
Officers	458	574	924
Engineers	35	62	159
Surgeons	63	98	164
Paymasters	42	72	119
CREW			
Deck officers	284	649	1,280
Under officers	1,459	2,401	5,558
Privates/seamen	8,043	11,922	19,978

> It is useful to note that as soon as the naval bill programme of 1900 has been carried through, that is to say in 1905, the strength of the Kaiser's fleet will be 60,000 men.

1 *When and how were the statistics collected? Who collected them?*

The German Admiralty, since these are official statistics.

2 *Is it likely that someone else working in exactly the same way would collect the same statistics?*

Yes. The statistics show the strength of the German Navy. These records would be carefully maintained by the Navy and only exaggerated in time of war!

3 *Are the statistics complete or only a sample of all the possible statistics which could have been recorded?*

They are complete for the years recorded. Statistics for the intervening years will be different.

4 *Who selected the statistics for use and how were they chosen?*

No information available.

5   *What do the statistics tell you about the past? What do they prove? If they are quoted to back up a statement do they really support the conclusions drawn from them by the writer?*

They show the extent of German rearmament and the beginnings of the naval arms race between Britain and Germany in the years immediately preceding the First World War. The statistics back up the statement that 'the German navy within this short period has increased threefold'.

6   *Are the statistics used to support any statement which may be biased or prejudiced?*

No.

EXERCISES AND ACTIVITIES

Draw graphs to show the growth of the Kaiser's navy in the years between 1881 and 1901.

Working as a Historian

SIMILARITIES AND DIFFERENCES

German barbed wire entanglements

Allied barbed wire entanglements. Both drawings date from the same year – 1916. In each case, the barbed wire protects a trench concealed behind the wire. Compare the two pictures. Can you pick out the trenches? What similarities are there? How do the two scenes differ from each other?

From *Sir Douglas Haig's Great Push*, Hutchinson

Similarity does not mean 'the same'. It means that things are alike in certain respects but not identical. This is an important difference. Two mill towns may look alike to an outsider but they may be very different places to the people who actually live there.

In fact every historical event is unique. There is nothing quite like it. This is why it is often much easier to detect differences than it is to find similarities. Nevertheless there are patterns in history. A revolution in one country may be followed by similar revolutions in neighbouring countries.

If you are asked to look for similarities and differences in history you may be asked to compare two or three written extracts or a number of pictures or photographs. You will need to pick out the important things that matter, not the minor details. If you jot down the main similarities and differences first of all, you can use these lists later on to help plan your essay.

EXERCISES AND ACTIVITIES

Study Sources A, B, C, D and the photographs. They show how people greeted the outbreak of the First World War in London and Berlin.

SOURCE A

A JOURNALIST IN LONDON

AUG: (Piccadilly Hotel) Was awakened by loud noises. Great crowds are parading the streets, exulting in the anticipation of war. This mafficking [rejoicing] for such universal tragedy makes me feel sad, and I am unable to sleep. Wasn't it Walpole who said: 'Yes! they are ringing their bells now; soon they will be wringing their hands!'? . . . I cannot sleep. They are going mad. Have they no imagination? They say war with Germany is inevitable. Possibly so – but why jubulate [rejoice] – how *can* they? . . . Can they not realize what war really means, these mad maffickers – what it means to women as well as men?

The Private Diaries of Sydney Moseley, Max Parrish, 1960

SOURCE B

A LONDON NEWSPAPER

A lady came out of the Palace, and announced that war had been declared. This was received with tremendous cheering, which grew into a deafening roar when King George, Queen Mary and the Prince of Wales appeared on the balcony shortly after eleven o'clock.

They looked down upon an extraordinary scene – a dense mass of excited people, many of whom had clambered on to the Victoria Memorial. As if by general accord, the cheers gave way to the singing of the National Anthem, which was taken up lustily by the whole throng.

For fully five minutes the Royal Party remained on the balcony. They retired amidst a perfect storm of cheering, and although the crowd subsequently began to melt away, thousands remained. They gew gradually less demonstrative, and it was noticeable that the news of the actual state of war had a sobering effect on many. Mafficking gave way to distinct seriousness.

Daily News and Leader, 5 August 1914

Crowds outside
Buckingham Palace,
London, August 1914

Crowds in the Unter
den Linden, Berlin,
August 1914

SOURCE C   A BRITISH JOURNALIST IN BERLIN

For two days I waited and watched. Up and down the wide road of Unter den Linden crowds paced incessantly by day and night singing the German war songs: 'Was blasen die Trompeten?' [Who blows the trumpet?] which is the finest; 'Deutschland, Deutschland ueber Alles,' [Germany, Germany above all] which comes next, and 'Die Wacht am Rhein,' [The Watch on the Rhine] which was the most popular ... Sometimes the Kaiser in full uniform swept along in his fine motor ... Cheered he was certainly, but everyone believed or knew that the Kaiser himself had never wished for war ... The most mighty storm of cheering was reserved for the Crown Prince, known to be at variance with his father in longing to test his imagined genius on the field. Him the people cheered, for they had never known war.

Henry W. Nevinson, *More Changes More Chances*,
James Nisbet, 1925

SOURCE D

A BRITISH WOMAN IN BERLIN

BERLIN, August 9th, 1914

The excitement and enthusiasm all over the city are enormous. The Kaiser is the most adored man of the moment, and during a great speech he delivered the other day on the balcony of the castle, in spite of the people standing densely thronged together, the silence was so great that one might have heard a pin fall. Certainly the whole nation are backing him this time, and if he has been criticized for his actions in the past, this war-cry is making him the most popular man in Germany.

Evelyn, Princess Blücher, *An English Wife in Berlin* Constable, 1921. [She and her German husband had been living in England but returned to Germany on 6 August 1914.]

1   *Use the master checklist on page 54 to check out these sources first of all. Are they primary sources? Are they eyewitness accounts? Which parts of these extracts are facts and which are opinions?*

2   *What were the similarities and differences between Berlin and London in the way in which people greeted the war?*

3   *Do any of the writers appear to be biased or prejudiced? The descriptions of Berlin were written by people who were British not German. Is there any sign that this may have affected the way in which they described the reactions of the Germans to the war?*

4   *Do the photographs opposite support or contradict the written sources? In what ways are these photographs similar?*

SOURCE E

Cover of the German magazine Jugend *issue No. 3, published in 1916*

SOURCE F

Cartoon in Punch *in March 1916 commemorating the epic battle at Verdun in which over 200 000 French soldiers were killed.*

5 *What are the similarities and differences between Sources E and F?*

6 *What is the link between Source E and Source C?*

7 *How did the artist who drew Source E expect the German people to react to his picture?*

8 *How did the* Punch *artist expect people in Britain to react?*

HOW THINGS CHANGE

28 July 1789: I am sure I need not tell you how much I have rejoiced at the Revolution which has taken place. I think of nothing else, and please myself with endeavouring to guess at some of the important consequences which must follow throughout Europe.

10 September 1792: How could we ever be so deceived in the character of the French nation as to think them capable of liberty! Wretches, who, after all their professions and boasts about liberty, and patriotism, and courage, and dying, and after taking oath after oath, at the very moment when their country is invaded and the enemy is marching through it unresisted, employ whole days in murdering women, and priests, and prisoners!

Letters from Sir Samuel Romilly to Etienne Dumont

These letters show how rapidly people change their attitudes to great events. How and why things change is of great interest to historians. Sometimes the changes are abrupt and clear cut, such as the sudden change in policy which happens when a revolutionary government seizes power. Changes of equal or greater significance in the lives of ordinary people also take place but often slowly over periods of many years.

Despite these changes many things, such as people's attitudes, customs and traditions, often remain much the same. This is called *continuity*. Change and continuity can both be identified when you make comparisons over a period of time.

Checklist — **Change**

Use these checkpoints if you are asked to identify changes which may have taken place.

1   *What was the nature of the change? Was it part of a much bigger change?*

2   *Was it an important and significant change? Did it affect everybody and almost every activity, like a political change, such as a revolution or a radically different government? Or did it just affect a section of the community, such as the effect of the means test in the 1930s on the unemployed?*

3   *Who or what benefited from the change? Who or what suffered from the change?*

4   *Did the change take place suddenly, rapidly, steadily, slowly, jerkily or imperceptibly?*

5   *Did the change affect people mainly because of its political effects, such as on relations with other countries? Or because of its social and economic effects, such as on health or industry?*

Going through the Checklist

BERLIN, November 8, 1918
I wonder what the result of the meeting of the delegates for an armistice today will be? . . . Every one expects that France will take her fill of revenge and make terms as hard as she can. Poor Germany is not in a position to resist any humiliation; she is completely exhausted.

Evening, November 9, 1918
Gebhardt and I were sitting quietly reading our papers, when at about two o'clock a perfect avalanche of humanity began to stream by our windows, walking quietly enough, many of them carrying red flags. . . .
    Our butler came in to announce that the Kaiser had abdicated. Tears came into both our eyes as we grasped the momentousness of the hour. . . . But it was not time to mourn for the individual, and our attention was soon fixed on what was passing outside our windows. There, evidently no one sorrowed at the loss of an emperor. There could hardly have been a greater air of rejoicing had Germany gained a great victory. More and more people came hurrying by, thousands of them densely packed together – men, women, soldiers, sailors.

Sunday morning, November 10, 1918
After we had all separated for the night, I lay awake, very tired. We were constantly disturbed by the sound of stray rifle-shots, and the feeling of uncertainty as to what was going on out there in the darkness of the huge city made sleep impossible. . . .

Princess Taxis rang us up to say that the new Socialist Chancellor, Ebert, has already threatened to resign as he cannot hold the people. . . . Amongst the aristocracy the grief at the breakdown of their country, more than at the personal fall of the Kaiser, is quite heart-rending to see. I have seen some of our friends, strong men, sit down and sob at the news, whilst others seemed to shrink to half their size and were struck dumb with pain.

Evelyn, Princess Blücher,
An English Wife in Berlin, Constable, 1921

Compare the extract above with the same writer's description of Berlin and the Kaiser at the start of the war only four years earlier (Source D on page 103).

1 *What was the nature of the change? Was it part of a much bigger change?*

It was a catastrophic change. Germany was exhausted; the armistice was about to be signed; the abdication of the Kaiser had brought to an end the Prussian monarchy and the German Empire. Germany was now a socialist republic. There was a very real possibility of a communist revolution, following the example of the Bolsheviks in Russia a year earlier.

2 *Was it an important and significant change? Did it affect everybody and almost every activity, or just a section of the community?*

Obviously it was an important and significant change, affecting everybody living in Germany. The autocratic rule of the Kaiser was at an end. No one knew what sort of government would take its place. The Princess Blücher was most disturbed at the uncertain future which lay ahead.

3 *Who or what benefited from the change? Who or what suffered from the change?*

The ordinary people, soldiers, sailors, strikers obviously thought that they would benefit. The aristocracy assumed that they would suffer.

4 *Did the change take place suddenly, rapidly, steadily, slowly, jerkily or imperceptibly?*

Suddenly with the collapse of the German war effort.

5 *Did the change affect people mainly because of its political effects? Or because of its social and economic effects?*

Mainly because of its political effects. It was too early to say what the social and economic effects would be.

EXERCISES AND ACTIVITIES

This Russian propaganda comic strip was published in *The Graphic* on 29 May 1920, less than three years after the start of the Bolshevik Revolution in Russia in November 1917.

*PETER WORKED HARD
ON HIS CORNFIELD*

*WHILE VASSILY WAS
DRUNK BOTH NIGHT
AND DAY*

Just at this time there fell upon Russia a great misfortune – the régime of the Soviet.

*A SOVIET ORATOR
ARRIVED ON THE
SCENE*

*AND FOR VASSILY
THERE CAME A HIGH
OLD TIME*

*BUT PETER WAS VERY
HARDLY DEALT WITH*

When a Leninite orator came down the drunken and ragged Vassily was the most enthusiastic of those present at the meeting, and was rewarded by being the first to receive authority over the village. . . . Vassily proclaimed the socialisation of property, and carried off all poor Peter's belongings.

*AND THIS IS WHAT HAPPENED TO THE VILLAGE
AFTER A MONTH OF THE BOLSHEVIK RÉGIME*

The result was that while some of the inhabitants deserted the village with their children, others lay in the cold grey earth. It was decreed that whoever had worked all his life with industrious hands was a harmful man. The cattle died and only the Soviet Committee and the dogs had enough to eat. Thus did the Bolshevik Vassily rule. While these pictures may be exaggerated, the story told in words is not; it is an accurate description of what has been happening all over Russia since the country had the tragic misfortune to fall under the tyranny of its new rulers. The people live under a perpetual Reign of Terror without parallel in Russian history. Murder stalks abroad in the land. Outrages are committed everywhere. The industrial life of the great nation has been paralysed. Famine has been added to the horrors of the people. Nothing is deemed sacred by the authors of this prolonged orgy of fiendish misrule.

The Graphic, 29 May 1920

1   *Examine this propaganda strip with the aid of the checklist for bias and prejudice on page 29. In particular, examine the way in which it was used by* The Graphic.

2   *What changes did the Bolshevik Revolution have on Russia according to the authors of this propaganda strip? Use the checklist printed on page 105 above to examine these changes.*

3   *Find out what really happened to agriculture in Russia in the first three years under communism. Was there any truth whatsoever in the propaganda strip? Was it 'an accurate description of what has been happening all over Russia since the country had the tragic misfortune to fall under the tyranny of its new rulers'?*

IMAGING THE PAST

Trying to imagine what it was like to live in the past is called historical *empathy*. It is a way of trying to understand why people behaved in the past in the way they did. Instead of judging their actions by our own standards we look at events and happenings through the eyes of the people living at that time.

Really understanding what happened in the past will only come about if you can set aside your own ideas and background and picture yourself in the past. How would you have behaved then? A good way of imagining yourself in the past is to think of everything in the present tense! What are your thoughts as you wait for the command 'to go over the top' at the battle of the Somme in 1916? What will you do if a Prussian officer takes over your house in Paris as a billet for his troops? Is it safe to walk near the Bastille at night?

Another way of getting a vivid picture of what it was really like to live in the past is to read accounts and stories which tell you how people spoke and how they behaved. Look closely at old pictures and especially at old photographs. When you see a photograph of a Victorian or an Edwardian town, for instance, try to imagine what it would have been like to be there when the photographer took the picture.

EXERCISES AND ACTIVITIES

Look at the following sources on trench warfare in the First World War (see also page 100).

SOURCE A

Inside a trench

SOURCE B   'A Working Party'

Three hours ago he blundered up the trench,
Sliding and poising, groping with his boots;
Sometimes he tripped and lurched against the walls
With hands that pawed the sodden bags of chalk.
He couldn't see the man who walked in front;
Only he heard the drum and rattle of feet
Stepping along barred trench boards, often splashing
Wretchedly where the sludge was ankle-deep.

Voices would grunt 'Keep to your right – make way!'
When squeezing past some men from the front line:
White faces peered, puffing a point of red;
Candles and braziers glinted through the chinks
And curtain-flaps of dug-outs; then the gloom
Swallowed his sense of sight; he stooped and swore
Because a sagging wire had caught his neck.

A flare went up; the shining whiteness spread
And flickered upward, showing nimble rats
And mounds of glimmering sand-bags, bleached with rain;
Then the slow silver moment died in the dark.
The wind came posting by with chilly gusts
And buffeting at corners, piping thin.
And dreary through the crannies; rifle-shots
Would split and crack and sing along the night,
And shells came calmly through the drizzling air
To burst with hollow bang below the hill.

                                        Siegfried Sassoon

SOURCE C   A LETTER FROM THE WESTERN FRONT

4 July 1916
B.E.F. [British Expeditionary Force]
France

From BOSKY

Am in a very comfortable DUG OUT with heaps of Head cover,
which is a great change from GALLIPOLI. But the mud is awful.
Have had two days of Torrential Rain which has flooded
everything. And the RATS ARE A CAUTION. I didn't believe
there were so many in the country. Black as well as brown. In fact
I'm fed up with the war. French life in France is not what it is
cracked up to be.

                            Peter Davies, *My Warrior Sons*,
                            edited by Guy Slater, 1973

SOURCE D

A bombing party off to the attack

SOURCE E

A LETTER HOME

December 14, 1916

According to the present routine, we stay in the front line eight days and nights; then go out for the same period. Each Company spends four days and four nights in the fire-trench before being relieved. The men are practically without rest. They are wet through much of the time. They are shelled and trench-mortared. They may not be hit, but they are kept in a perpetual state of unrest and strain. They work all night and every night, and a good part of each day, digging and filling sandbags, and repairing the breaches in the breastworks; – that is when they are not on sentry. The temperature is icy. They have not even a blanket. The last two days it has been snowing. They cannot move more than a few feet from their posts: therefore, except when they are actually digging, they cannot keep themselves warm by exercise; and, when they try to sleep, they freeze. At present they are getting a tablespoon of rum to console them, once in three days.

Rowland Feilding, *War Letters to a Wife*,
The Medici Society, 1929

SOURCE F

A British officer leading his section over the top on the first day of the battle of the Somme, 1 July 1916

SOURCE G

'The Sentry'

We'd found an old Boche dug-out, and he knew,
And gave us hell, for shell on frantic shell
Hammered on top, but never quite burst through.
Rain, guttering down in waterfalls of slime,
Kept slush waist-high and rising hour by hour,
And choked the steps too thick with clay to climb.

Wilfred Owen

SOURCE H

Painting from The Sphere *for 5 August 1916 showing a British officer leading his section across no man's land towards the enemy trenches*

1   *Use the checklists on pages 54, 80 and 91 to check through these extracts and the accompanying pictures.*

2   *Imagine that you are a soldier fighting in the trenches in 1916. What do you look like? What clothes are you wearing? When did you last wash or eat? What can you smell? What can you see and hear? Imagine what the trench looks like and what it is like to live there for several days at a time. What do you feel like when it is pouring with rain? What is it like in the middle of the night? What is it like in icy weather or when there is heavy snow? What do you feel like before making a raid across the lines in the middle of the night? What is it like 'to go over the top'? Describe your life in the trenches in a series of letters home or as a diary.*

CAUSE AND CONSEQUENCE

Punch cartoon dated 3 August 1889, almost exactly 25 years before the outbreak of the First World War. Grandma' Victoria – 'Now Willie dear, you've plenty of soldiers at home; look at these pretty ships. I'm sure you'll be pleased with them!'

VISITING GRANDMAMMA

The German Kaiser, William II, was Queen Victoria's grandson. His proposals to expand the German navy (see statistics on page 98) were regarded by the British Government as a serious threat to the supremacy of the Royal Navy. One consequence was an arms race. Britain retaliated by building super battleships, called Dreadnoughts. Rearmament was one of the contributory factors leading to the outbreak of war in 1914.

Whenever we look at how things change (see pages 104–8) we also look at the causes and consequences of making those changes. Scientists in certain subjects, such as physics and chemistry, can usually find out for certain why a change occurs. They can repeat an experiment over and over again until they are satisfied with the result. As a result, they know that if they repeat the cause (such as adding sulphuric acid to zinc) they will always get the same result or consequence (zinc sulphate and hydrogen). In history there is no such certainty.

Politicians argue that in appearing to give in to Hitler at Munich in 1938 (see pages 55–9), the British prime minister, Neville Chamberlain, only encouraged the Nazis to invade Poland in 1939. A policy like this, of giving way to a dictator, is called *appeasement*. Munich has since been used as a reason for acting toughly today. In other words, many politicians believe that aggression is the inevitable consequence of a policy of appeasement.

In fact, the Munich Crisis was unique. It is by no means certain that a similar consequence would follow in different circumstances, with another dictator, at another date, in another country. History is not like that. It can show people what happened in the past. It can teach them to learn from their past mistakes. But it cannot lay down strict laws like those you may have learned in science.

Checklist — **Cause and Consequence**

Use these checkpoints when you study cause and consequence.

1   *What are the suggested effects and consequences?*

2   *Are these effects and consequences facts which can be proved or disproved? Or are they opinions?*

3   *What causes of these effects and consequences have been given?*

4   *Which of these causes can be backed up by facts and evidence? Can they be proved or disproved?*

John Bull (Britain) links hands with France, Japan and Russia. What cause and what consequence are illustrated by this picture printed in The Graphic *on 7 September 1907?*

Going through the Checklist

Exactly what was the real cause of the war no one seems to know, although it is discussed night and day. One thing grows clearer to me every day: neither the people here nor there [in Britain] wished for war, but here they are now being carried off their legs with patriotism, at seeing so many enemies on every side. It is said in England that Germany provoked the war, and here they emphatically deny it. To me it seems that Europe was thirsting for war, and that the armies and navies were no longer to be restrained. Certainly here, the militarists grew weary of the long lazy peace as they called it, and if the Kaiser had not proclaimed war, he would have been in a precarious position.

> Evelyn, Princess Blücher, *An English Wife in Berlin*,
> Constable, 1921

1 *What are the suggested effects and consequences?*

The outbreak of the First World War.

2 *Are these effects and consequences facts which can be proved or disproved? Or are they opinions?*

Facts.

3 *What causes of these effects and consequences have been given?*

That the militarists in the armies and navies of Europe were thirsting for war and could no longer be restrained. In other words, that the arms race was a major cause of the war.

4 *Which of these causes can be backed up by facts and evidence? Can they be proved or disproved?*

It is easy enough to quote facts which show the extent of the arms build-up before 1914 but it is not easy to show that this is the reason why war broke out. That some people welcomed the chance to go to war has already been shown in the extracts and photographs on pages 101–3.

EXERCISES AND ACTIVITIES

Read this extract from the diary of Benjamin Moran, an American diplomat based in London during the Indian Mutiny (1857).

Thursday 10 September 1857: On reaching the Legation this morning I found the Rev L.G. Hay, an American Presbyterian Missionary from Allahabad, India, waiting for me. He was present there at the mutinous outbreak and gave me some thrilling details of the murders. . . . All the whites went early to the fort, but even there the arrogance of the English character exhibited itself at that trying time. His wife and self were two days and nights exposed in the open air under tents of his own while plenty of room remained unoccupied in the fort. . . . The confusion and alarm of the Eng. were frightful. All fellow-feeling for a time was lost; and some *ladies* and *gentlemen* displayed an amount of selfishness and indifference towards their countrymen & women of the basest character. Their conduct was no matter who suffers so we are saved . . .

He thinks the Moslems are at the bottom of the outbreak, backed by the higher caste Hindus. The followers of Mohammed want to rule India, & seeing England weak and wavering they have instigated [encouraged] the Sepoys [Indian-born soldiers], of whom the India Company has always been afraid. . . . Arrogance, ill-treatment of the natives, bad morals and fear of the Sepoys on the part of the East India Co., Mr Hay thinks have had their share in producing the rebellion. Good management would have prevented it all.

The Journal of Benjamin Moran,
edited by Sarah Agnes Wallace and
Frances Elma Gillespie, University of Chicago, 1948

1　*Go through the master checklist printed on page 54 and the checklist printed on page 114.*

2　*What were the suggested causes of the Indian Mutiny?*

3　*Are there any particular advantages to be gained from looking at events in British history through the eyes of an American?*

'The storming of the Cashmere Gate in Delhi during the Indian Mutiny.' The Illustrated London News, *28 November 1857.*

SELECTING RELEVANT INFORMATION

Selecting relevant information means selecting only those facts, opinions, judgements and ideas which relate specifically to the subject you are studying.

It is interesting to know that Florence Nightingale was called Florence because she was born in Florence in Italy. But this information is irrelevant if you are studying her work as a nurse. It is relevant, however, if you are writing the story of her life. It is easy to be side-tracked in this way. This is why you should always try to make an effort to stick to the subject. Only use information which throws light on your topic.

EXERCISES AND ACTIVITIES

The following extract is from a newspaper account of the trial of a young man who had been accused of breaking the new Combination Laws in 1825. These new Combination Laws actually made it easier for trade unions to operate. The old Combination Acts, passed in 1799 and 1800, had effectively banned trade unions since workers could be sent to prison for attending strike meetings or for 'combining' with other workers to force an employer to raise wages or improve working conditions. In this account of the trial of Robert Ford you can find out how the new Combination Laws worked.

> Friday, a young man, named Robert Ford, a journeyman shoemaker, was brought up on a warrant charged under the New Act, with endeavouring by threats and intimidation, to prevent one George Turner, from returning to his work. It appeared that all the men in the employment of Mr. Ashenden, a boot and shoemaker, at Hampstead, struck for wages about a fortnight ago. Among the rest were the above-named Ford and Turner. The latter, however, was compelled by the rest to strike against his will; and when the whole party were assembled at a public house debating the matter, he said he was sorry he had left his work, and would return to it; upon which Ford, who was one of the most active promoters of the 'strike', swore that if he did he would drag him through a pond. This was the 'threat and intimidation' complained of.
>
> Ford, in defence, said he made use of no threat. The words he made use of were these: 'If you return to your work, you ought to be dragged through a pond.'
>
> Mr. Halls [the magistrate] said, Turner had sworn otherwise.
>
> Mr. Ashenden said, he should not have brought the prisoner here, but this was not a solitary instance of his having used threats to other men.

Mr. Halls said, he certainly should put the act in force against the prisoner. Even now he did it with reluctance, but some check must be put upon the dangerous spirit which seemed to prevail. For the instruction of those whom he saw within hearing he would read that part of one clause of the recent act, which applied to the present case. It stated 'that if any person shall by violence to the person or property, or by threats or intimidation, or by molesting or in any way obstructing another, force or endeavour to force, any journeyman, manufacturer, etc., to depart from his business, or to return his work before it is finished, or preventing any person from returning to his work, etc., every person so offending, or aiding, or assisting therein, shall be imprisoned for any period not exceeding three months.' The act left it to the discretion of the Magistrates whether the hard labour should be added to the imprisonment. The prisoner was sentenced to one month's imprisonment but not to hard labour.

The Age, Sunday 17 July 1825

1 *Is this a primary source? Is it an eyewitness account? Go through the master checklist on page 54.*

2 *Why was Robert Ford sent to prison? Was it because he went on strike or because he organised the strike? Search through this passage and find the relevant part of the evidence and the relevant part of the Combination Laws which sent him to prison for one month.*

3 *Which of the following did the new Combination Laws prohibit:*

  (a) going on strike

  (b) standing in the path of someone wishing to return to work

  (c) threatening a fellow worker

  (d) peaceful picketing (i.e. asking fellow workers not to go back to work)

  (e) erecting a barrier across the entrance to the works to stop people returning to work?

FOR AND AGAINST

A *reasoned argument* is one in which each stage of the argument follows from the preceding one. It uses good reasons to argue the case for or against. The reasons are good because they are based on known facts rather than on bias, prejudice or inaccurate facts.

Use this checklist when you examine the arguments in any historical source.

Checklist — A Reasoned Argument

1   *List the arguments* for.

2   *List the arguments* against.

3   *Which of these arguments are based on facts and which are opinions? Which can be proved? Which are unprovable?*

4   *Which arguments seem to you to be backed up by the most convincing evidence? Which arguments are weak and unconvincing? Which side has the better case?*

Going through the Checklist

The extracts that follow are from an article by Frederick Ryland in *The Girl's Own Paper*, in 1896, discussing the arguments for and against votes for women. This was several years before the founding of the suffragette movement.

EXTRACT A

Men and women certainly do not entirely understand each other's point of view, and there are many questions, some great and some small, in which women as a rule take a line of their own.

EXTRACT B

Then there is the argument for justice. Why should a person otherwise qualified be refused a vote simply on the ground of sex? Mr A. at No. 1 has a vote; Mrs B at No. 2, with equal education, and an equal stake in the country, is refused a vote, merely because she is a woman. This seems on the face of it to be an outrage on fairness. But, as a matter of fact, things are usually worse, since Mrs B's gardener or coachman will probably have a vote, while she is without one.

EXTRACT C

Suppose, for instance, the vast majority of men were in favour of a war with Russia, and the women vetoed it, or vice versa; in either case it would be felt that as the men supply by far the greater part of the blood and the treasure which would be spent on a war, and are out of all comparison in a better position to judge of the effect of such a war on the honour, welfare, and commerce of the country, with them must rest the final decision.

Frederick Ryland, 'Politics for Girls: Female Suffrage',
The Girl's Own Paper, 16 May 1896

1 *List the arguments* for.

    (a) Women have their own opinions and these should be heard.

    (b) It is unfair to give the vote to men and not to women with the same qualifications.

2 *List the arguments* against.

    (c) Women should not be able to vote on issues which might result in a war which men would have to fight and finance.

    (d) Men are better able to judge the effect of such a war on the country.

3 *Which of these arguments are based on facts and which are opinions? Which can be proved? Which are unprovable?*

Arguments (a), (b) and (c) are based on provable facts – (a) women do have their own opinions, (b) some women in 1896 did have the same voting qualifications as men, (c) in 1896 men fought wars not women [but note that women directly and indirectly helped to finance them]. Argument (d) is Frederick Ryland's unprovable opinion.

4 *Which arguments seem to you to be backed up by the most convincing evidence? Which arguments are weak and unconvincing? Which side has the better case?*

Arguments (a) and (b) are backed by convincing evidence. There is no logical answer to either argument.

Argument (c) is arrogant nonsense. As Ryland knew, 'by far the greater part of the blood' spent on a war in 1896 would have been given *not* by men entitled to vote *but* by young men under 21 who were unable to vote, and by other young men over 21 who were disqualified from voting because they were not householders. Argument (d), that men can better judge the effect of a war, is rubbish if the insane celebrations in August 1914 are any guide (see pages 101–3).

Lady Dorothy Howard arguing the cause of the suffragettes at a political meeting in 1908

EXERCISES AND ACTIVITIES

Sources A, B, C and D are about the rights and wrongs of imperialism. Go through each extract using the checklist printed above. Write a reasoned essay explaining the arguments used by these writers in attacking and defending imperialism.

SOURCE A

WILLIAM COBBETT in 1808

16 April 1808
What right, in God's name, what right have we to do this? How is it possible for us to justify our conduct, upon any principle of morality? Conquests in India are not at all necessary either to our safety or our comfort. There is no glory attending such conquests and their accompanying butcheries. We must be actuated by a sheer love of gain; a sheer love of plunder.

The Opinions of William Cobbett,
edited by G. D. H. and M. Cole, 1944

SOURCE B

RICHARD COBDEN in 1849 and 1857

10 January 1849
People tell me I want to abandon our colonies; but I say, do you intend to hold your colonies by the sword, by armies, and ships of war? That is not a permanent hold upon them.

16 October 1857
I do not believe in the possibility of the Crown governing India under the control of Parliament . . . Hindoostan [i.e. India] must be ruled by those who live on that side of the globe. Its people will prefer to be ruled badly – *according to our notions* – by its own colour, kith and kin, than to submit to the humiliation of being better governed by a succession of transient [temporary] intruders from the antipodes [i.e. Britain].

SOURCE C

LORD LUGARD in 1893

The 'Scramble for Africa' by the nations of Europe – an incident without parallel in the history of the world – was due to the growing commercial rivalry, which brought home to civilised nations the vital necessity of securing the only remaining fields for industrial enterprise and expansion. . . . It is well, then, to realise that it is for our *advantage* – and not alone at the dictate of duty – that we have undertaken responsibilities in East Africa. It is in order to foster the growth of the trade of this country, and to find an outlet for our manufacturers and our surplus energy, that our far-seeing statesmen and our commercial men advocate colonial expansion. . . .

There are some who say we have no *right* in Africa at all, that 'it belongs to the natives.' I hold that our right is the necessity that is upon us to provide for our evergrowing population – either by opening new fields for emigration, or by providing work and employment which the development of over-sea extension entails – and to stimulate trade by finding new markets, since we know what misery trade depression brings at home.

While thus serving our own interests as a nation, we may, by selecting men of the right stamp for the control of new territories, bring at the same time many advantages to Africa. Nor do we deprive the natives of their birthright of freedom, to place them under a foreign yoke. It has ever been the kcy-note of British colonial method to rule through and by the natives, and it is this method, in contrast to the arbitrary and uncompromising rule of Germany, France, Portugal, and Spain, which has been the secret of our success as a colonising nation, and has made us welcomed by tribes and peoples in Africa, who ever rose in revolt against the other nations named.

Lord Lugard, *The Rise of Our East African Empire*,
William Blackwood, 1893

Cartoon from Punch, *30 September 1882. To which of the four sources, A, B, C, D, does this cartoon relate? What was the artist's intention in drawing this cartoon?*

THE LION'S JUST SHARE

SOURCE D

J.A. HOBSON in 1902

What is the direct economic outcome of Imperialism? A great expenditure of public money upon ships, guns, military and naval equipment and stores ... enormous profits when a war, or an alarm of war, occurs ... more posts for soldiers and sailors and in the diplomatic and consular services ... markets for certain classes of exports, and some protection and assistance for British trades in these manufactures; employment for engineers, missionaries, speculative miners, ranchers, and other emigrants. ...

The decades of Imperialism have been prolific in wars. ... Every one of the steps of expansion in Africa, Asia, and the Pacific has been accompanied by bloodshed; each Imperialist power keeps an increasing army available for foreign service . . . fighting has been well-nigh incessant . . . Apart from the enmity of France and Germany, the main cause of the vast armaments which are draining the resources of most European countries is their conflicting interests in territorial and commercial expansion.

J. A. Hobson, *Imperialism: A Study*, 1902

REACHING A CONCLUSION

In an examination, or in a special study, you will often have to reach a conclusion. This is a summing up of what you know about a topic. A good conclusion will balance different opinions and arguments against each other and then state clearly the verdict of the writer. A good conclusion will be supported by facts and historical evidence (if this is available). It will avoid making generalisations based on only one or two examples.

EXERCISES AND ACTIVITIES

1   *Examine the sources A, B, C, D, E which follow, testing each with the checklist printed on page 54. In particular, take note which are primary and which are secondary sources.*

2   *Source A below was written at the end of 1916. Sir Douglas Haig, the commander of the British army, sums up the results achieved in the battle of the Somme, the world's bloodiest battle. Use Sources B, C, D and E which follow to say why you agree or disagree with his conclusion. In particular, check each of his 'three main objects' against the facts quoted by the other sources.*

3   *Write your own conclusion, based on Sir Douglas Haig's statement, but correcting it in the light of the information you obtain from these other sources.*

SOURCE A

By the third week in November the three main objects with which we had commenced our offensive had already been achieved: Verdun had been relieved; the main German forces had been held on the Western Front; and the enemy's strength had been very considerably worn down. 'Any one of these three results,' writes Sir Douglas Haig, 'is in itself sufficient to justify the Somme battle. The attainment of all three of them affords ample compensation for the splendid efforts of our troops and for the sacrifices made by ourselves and our Allies. They have brought us a long step forward towards the final victory of the Allied cause.'

Sir Douglas Haig's Great Push, Hutchinson
[no date given but almost certainly published in 1917]

SOURCE B   It is claimed that the battle of the Somme destroyed the old
                                        German Army by killing off its best officers and men. It killed off
                                        far more of our best and of the French best.

                                                                    David Lloyd George, *War Memoirs*, Odhams Press, 1933
                                                                    (British Prime Minister from 1916 to the end of the War.)

SOURCE C   The battle with the greatest recorded number of military casualties
                                        was the First Battle of thc Somme, France 1 July to 19 Nov 1916,
                                        with 1,043,896 – Allied 623,907 (of which 419,654 were British) and
                                        419,989 German.

                                                                                         Guinness Book of Records 1987

SOURCE D   In the Somme fighting of 1916 there was a spirit of heroism which
                                        was never again found in the division . . . the men in 1918 had not
                                        the temper, the hard bitterness and spirit of sacrifice of their
                                        predecessors.

                                                                            Die 27 Infanterie Division im Weltkrieg
                                                            (the Official History of the German 27th Infantry Division)

SOURCE E   . . . at a conference on February 14th, an agreement was reached by
                                        which Haig accepted Joffre's plan for the Somme offensive –
                                        dated for July 1st . . . the offensive was only a few weeks old when
                                        the story was spread . . . that Haig was throughout aiming at a
                                        campaign of attrition [wearing down the enemy] and had not
                                        dreamt of a 'breakthrough'. This denial was vehemently maintained
                                        for years, long after the war; it forms one of the most elaborate
                                        perversions of historical truth that has come to light . . . publication
                                        of the Official History in 1932 . . . revealed that . . . Haig . . . both
                                        sought and believed in a breakthrough.

                                                                            B. H. Liddell Hart, *History of the First World War*,
                                                                                                                Cassell, 1970

                        Notes

                        (a) A 'campaign of attrition' means wearing the enemy down – you lose
                            soldiers but expect the enemy to lose even more.
                        (b) The battle of Verdun was fought between French and German armies
                            from 21 February to 16 December 1916.
                        (c) The front line at the end of November 1916 was still much the same as
                            it had been on 1 July 1916. The battle of the Somme had little effect in
                            hastening the end of the war, which did not come until two years later
                            in November 1918.

Summary Checklists

Checklist — Documentary Evidence

1   What does the source tell you about the past?

2   What is the origin of the source? What type of evidence is it (e.g. diary, letter, newspaper report)? Is it likely to be reliable?

3   Why was the source written? Was it written to justify the writer's actions? Does the writer try to take credit for successes which other people claim for themselves? Does the writer put the blame for failures on to other people?

4   When was the source written? Is it a primary source dating from the time of the event which it describes? Or is it a secondary source?

5   Is there any clue or statement to show that it is an actual eyewitness account? Was the writer in a good position to say what happened? Does the source agree with other eyewitness accounts of the same event? Are there any reasons for thinking the eyewitness cannot be trusted entirely?

6   If the source was written years after the event is there any reason to doubt the accuracy of the writer's memory?

7   Which parts of the extract seem to you to be opinions and not facts which can be proved right or wrong? Are the opinions based on facts or on prejudice? Has the writer used words of approval or disapproval, or colourful or exaggerated phrases, to try to influence the reader?

8   Does the author show any other signs of bias or prejudice? Does the writer appear to take sides in an argument?

9   Are there any obvious mistakes or errors of fact in the extract? Which statements are supported by facts you know about from other sources? Does anything in the extract contradict other sources or facts which you already know to be true?

10 Does the account give a distorted view of events which actually occurred? Has the author left out facts which tell a different story? Is any part of the extract an obvious lie or exaggeration? Are there any obvious gaps in the evidence, such as missing dates, facts or personalities?

Checklist — **Pictures from the Past**

1   *Does the picture attempt to portray realistically people, events, buildings, etc., or does it poke fun at them by means of a cartoon or an exaggerated drawing (called a caricature)?*

2   *What does the picture show? What does it tell us about the past?*

3   *When was the picture drawn? Was it drawn at roughly the same time as the event or feature it depicts? Is it a primary source? If no date is given can you estimate roughly the date when it was drawn from the clothes worn by the people in the picture, from styles of vehicles (such as motor cars), or from other clues?*

4   *Why was the picture drawn or painted? Was it simply an illustration (e.g. to accompany a news item or to illustrate a book), or is there any reason to think the artist was using the picture to make you feel in a certain way about the events or people depicted? For instance, was it drawn or painted to make you want to protest against an injustice, or to feel excited, or sad, or nostalgic for an old way of life, or patriotic, or self-satisfied, or envious of someone else's way of life?*

5   *Does the picture show something which could not be shown in any other way, such as the interior of a courtroom where photographs are not permitted?*

6   *Even if it looks like a realistic picture is there any reason to think it is a product of the artist's imagination rather than a portrayal of an actual scene or event?*

7   *If the picture is a cartoon, what was the artist getting at? What does the cartoon tell you about the topic, events or people portrayed? What does it tell you about the attitude of the artist who drew the cartoon or of the magazine which published it?*

Checklist — **Relics from the Past**

1   *What was the purpose of the object or building you are studying? What was it used for? Why was it built or made?*

2   *Can you date the object or building either exactly or approximately?*

3   *Where is it situated now or where was it found? Where did it come from originally?*

4   *What does it tell us about people in the past?*

Checklist — **Photographs**

1   *What does the photograph show? What does it tell us about the past?*

2   *When and where was the photograph taken? If no date is given, use clues to estimate the date.*

3   *Why was the photograph taken? Is there any reason to think the photographer chose a viewpoint or a subject to make us feel in a certain way about the event or people depicted?*

4   *Is there any sign that the people in the photograph are posing for the photographer? Were they aware of the camera? Does this make any difference to the value of the photograph?*

5   *Is there any reason to think that the photograph is not a typical example of what it appears to show? Is there any reason to think that it may have been altered in any way?*

Checklist — **Statistics**

1   *When and how were the statistics collected? Who collected them? Were they in a position to collect accurate or reliable statistics? Can we be certain they are not guesses, estimates, approximations or even lies?*

2   *Is it likely that someone else working in exactly the same way would collect the same statistics? If not, why not?*

3   *Are the statistics complete or only a sample of all the possible statistics which could have been recorded?*

4   *Who selected the statistics for use and how were they chosen?*

5   *What do the statistics tell you about the past? What do they prove? If they are quoted to back up a statement do they really support the conclusions drawn from them by the writer?*

6   *Are the statistics used to support a statement which may be biased or prejudiced?*

7   *If averages are used, do they mean anything? See if you can find out how they were calculated?*

Checklist — Change

1   What was the nature of the change? Was it part of a much bigger change?

2   Was it an important and significant change? Did it affect everybody and almost every activity, or just a section of the community?

3   Who or what benefited from the change? Who or what suffered from the change?

4   Did the change take place suddenly, rapidly, steadily, slowly, jerkily or imperceptibly?

5   Did the change affect people mainly because of its political effects, such as on relations with other countries? Or because of its social and economic effects, such as on health or industry?

Checklist — Cause and Consequence

1   What are the suggested effects and consequences?

2   Are these effects and consequences facts which can be proved or disproved? Or are they opinions?

3   What causes of these effects and consequences have been given?

4   Which of these causes can be backed up by facts and evidence? Can they be proved or disproved?

Checklist — A Reasoned Argument

1   List the arguments for.

2   List the arguments against.

3   Which of these arguments are based on facts and which are opinions? Which can be proved? Which are unprovable?

4   Which arguments seem to you to be backed up by the most convincing evidence? Which arguments are weak and unconvincing? Which side has the better case?

Checklist — **The Link with the Past**

1 Find out if there are any features, such as buildings, monuments, street names or house names near your home which link up in some way with the topic.

2 Which of your living relatives (if any) were alive for part of the time covered by the topic? What do they remember about this period?

3 What things from the past can you find in your local museum or library which link up with this topic?

Index

CONCEPTS, SKILLS AND SOURCES

THEMES IN BRITISH AND EUROPEAN HISTORY